IT'S PERSONAL (NOT) PERSONNEL

Leadership Lessons for the Battlefield and the Boardroom

PRAISE FOR
IT'S PERSONAL, NOT PERSONNEL: LEADERSHIP LESSONS FOR THE BATTLEFIELD AND THE BOARDROOM

───────────

"As a female Army Chaplain joining one of the Army's most prestigious brigades, I arrived with reservations about my abilities to serve in a male-dominated organization. Colonel Campbell immediately dispelled my concerns. His refreshing leadership was exceptional and relevant for an organization under enormous stress. In a world where people climb over others to excel, his unique ability to empower people to be their very best is what sets this leader apart."

Chaplain (Major) Jennifer Cooper
United States Army

"I am a better soldier, husband and man because of Colonel Rob Campbell's leadership. Unlike any leader I have served with in 24 years, he helped me and many others identify their personal and professional deficiencies and overcome them. Across his vast organization, every member knew investing in our people was our top priority. I'm forever indebted to Rob Campbell."

Lieutenant Colonel Jay Harty
United States Army

"While the importance of people is noted throughout business literature, in contrast to many others, Colonel Rob Campbell is a practitioner who always placed people in the forefront of the organizations he led. The success of his unique approach can be seen in his organizations' superior performance. If results matter for your organization, this is the book to read!"

James W. Derleth, PhD

Senior Interagency Training Advisor
U.S. Army - Joint Multinational Readiness Center
Hohenfels, Germany

"People are the engine that makes your business run smoothly. Not getting personal means leadership failure, and that's no way to run a business. Rob provides a personal approach to leadership that's unparalleled. Everyone should read this book!"

Jeffrey Hayzlett

Primetime TV & Radio Host, Speaker,
Author and Part-Time Cowboy

"Rob's transparency as a leader, personal investment in his people and leadership methods are a great model for any executive. Worth reading for sure."

Cameron Herold

Founder of the COO Alliance
Author of Double Double, Meetings Suck,
and The Miracle Morning for Entrepreneurs

MAKE IT

↓

IT'S PERSONAL !
(NOT) PERSONNEL

Leadership Lessons for the Battlefield and the Boardroom

Colonel Rob Campbell
UNITED STATES ARMY, RETIRED

It's Personal, Not Personnel:
Leadership Lessons for the Battlefield and the Boardroom

Copyright 2017 by Rob Campbell

All rights reserved.

Published by Silver Tree Publishing, a division of Silver Tree Communications, LLC (Kenosha, WI).

www.SilverTreeCommunications.com

Editing by:
Cathy Fyock
Hilary Jastram
Kate Colbert

Cover design and typesetting by:
Courtney Hudson

First edition, October 2017

ISBN: 978-0-9991491-2-6

Library of Congress Control Number: 2017955501

Created in the United States of America

DEDICATION

To my wife Leslie and sons Robbie and Louden for investing in me with their love. And to my father Bruce M. Campbell, a true gentleman who would treat a cashier the same as a CEO.

ACKNOWLEDGMENTS

I've rarely ever done anything by myself, this book included. It was only made possible by countless people who invested in me as a leader and a person. Their impact on me extends far beyond the book's pages.

My deep love and respect goes out to the entire Hamp family, especially my in-laws Conrad and Theresa, Aunt Mary Campbell, and my sister Melissa Dilorenzo. Thanks as well to Laura and Scott Russell, and Ron and Kathy Grein.

I'm indebted to great leaders like General Tom Hill; Lieutenant General Jim Terry; Major Generals Jeff Smith, Drew Poppas, Bryan Owens, Mike Howard, and Mark Stammer; Colonels Jon Laurich, George Oliver, Mace Crowe, Tim Scully and Jeff Martindale; Lieutenant Colonel Tim Leroux; Major Mike Brettmann; and Dr. Jim Derleth.

For inspiring and encouraging me to write this book, my wife Leslie, Brandon Turner and Jim Hughes. I had a great team of friends and colleagues who bravely ventured into the early stages of the book to help make it a finished product. Thank you, Scott Campbell, Fred Johnson, Diane Bailey-Boulet, Byrd Baggett, Cathy Fyock and Kate Colbert.

Huge credit to the brigade personnel section of the 1st Brigade, 101st Airborne Division. They took our investing-in-people approach and championed it.

Lastly, to the United States Army for 27 incredible years and to the countless soldiers I was privileged to serve with in peacetime and in war, a few of whom paid the ultimate price for our country's freedom. You'll live forever in my heart.

TABLE OF CONTENTS

FOREWORD

I heard a historian once speak on the significance of the Higgins boat, which delivered the soldiers of the Allied Expeditionary Force to the beaches of Normandy, France, and how that boat helped win the war. While I agree with the premise, the reality is that it was the *people* in the boat who won the war — the boat was merely a conveyance. People are the very lifeblood of our organizations and it is the responsibility of every leader to care for or, as Rob Campbell effectively states, *invest in them.*

In every one of my leadership, speaking or teaching engagements in a career spanning 50 years, I always share with the audience what has given my life meaning — that is making a positive difference in the lives of others. If I can enrich your life, and you in turn can enrich another's, what a better world we would live in — one person at a time. Leadership is a very personal endeavor and Rob captures this eloquently in the pages ahead. You won't find a more authentic, transparent and effective leader than Rob Campbell. I have personally watched him lead and marveled at his ability to create organizational success through his unwavering focus on investing in people. He simply has a gift and the Army was the beneficiary of his talents for many years. Now, with this book, leaders of all organizations can benefit, as the Army did, emulating Rob's methods. This is a must-read book for anyone who leads people. It's a must-read because Rob gets it. First and foremost, *it's about making people better people* and demonstrating that you desire to lead and nurture them. The title says it all — it's personal, not personnel.

General James T. Hill
United States Army Retired

INTRODUCTION

"Caring about the happiness of others,
we find our own."
— Plato —

Consider the tale of two Kens. Ken #1 applied for a different job after he and his fiancée moved to a new area together. He was looking for a role that would feed his passion for art and for the development of children. He interviewed for a position to establish and lead a new afterschool program at a high school in the local area. There he would have an opportunity to flourish, creating and developing and making a difference in the lives of teenagers. As had happened with many of the positions he'd applied for, communication from the would-be employer was poor, so he had to follow up to learn if he was being considered. When he finally contacted the school principal, he learned that he was hired. Equipped with a cursory understanding of his role, having interviewed and read the job description, Ken set to work.

On day one, he arrived to find that he was going to occupy a desk in a large storage closet near the noisy cafeteria. There were no resources for him like a computer, printer, email or a building access badge. Only a few people in the school knew who he was and why he was there. Being new and having overcome greater obstacles, he didn't complain; rather, he began building a program and creating a workable space to facilitate his duties. Ken was never given any sort of initial counseling — formal or informal mentoring, coaching or guidance — for his role in the organization. His boss sent an email to all her subordinates stating, "My door is open to any employee any time." (That seemed to be code for: *"People are not my priority. Come by if you have an issue and if I am not busy I will make time to listen."*) Eventually Ken would be given resources and become known by other school team members. He would develop a great reputation among his students' parents and his fellow workers, but had to struggle to achieve that. He was never given any counseling, mentoring or guidance throughout the year and when his new afterschool program was certified ahead of schedule and lauded by the inspectors, he was never recognized or rewarded.

Now meet Ken #2. Ken #2 experiences a thorough interview process where a team asks about his values and goals to ensure alignment with the school. He is informed about the selection process, and the principal calls him personally to congratulate him on being accepted into the team. Ken enters the school on his first day experiencing a formal welcome by its members. His boss meets with him briefly and thanks him for his candor in the interview process and describes briefly what she enjoyed most about what Ken had to share. She hands Ken her biography sketch, which describes who she is as a person (see a sample bio sketch on page 92), and his first counseling form. That form includes the school's vision and an outline of expectations for his position. The principal informs Ken that this is his read-ahead for his initial counseling, which will occur within the week.

In the counseling session a week later, the principal spends the preponderance of time asking questions about Ken's family, his interests and passions and if he has any long-term personal and professional goals. She tells Ken that she desires to get to know him personally and wants to have a very honest conversation when they meet for counseling about his strengths and weaknesses, goal achievement and how he feels about his role in the organization. Periodic counseling occurs where Ken and his boss spend quality time in a closed session talking about where he might be struggling, where he is in pursuit of his goals and how his boss can help him succeed. He sees his boss on numerous occasions and notices how engaged she is when she visits, asking questions about his family, questioning him about current and enduring priorities, and asking what he needs. Ken receives a birthday and anniversary card from his boss. He is recognized in front of his teammates with a certificate for his performance when his new afterschool program achieves certification.

At the end of the year, Ken receives his formal evaluation from his boss in another closed-door session and has time to review and discuss it. Ken is not surprised by the assessment because he and his supervisor have been talking about this in regular counseling sessions during the school year. He leaves the session and ends the year in his new job having grown professionally and personally, and feeling that his employer sees him as a worthy investment. His loyalty to his boss and school increases and he recommits himself to becoming better and better each day. Ken #2 has an immeasurably more positive experience than Ken #1, even though they have the very same job.

Does the story of Ken #1 sound familiar to you in any way? Have you experienced this? Do people experience this in your organization? If the answer to any of these is "Yes," or if you desire to create an environment like the alternative one — the positive experience of Ken #2 — then you need this book.

What I described at the start of this introduction is a true story. Ken #1 is not alone. By and large, we leaders (I include myself for the times I got it wrong) pay lip service to investing in people. We manage (not lead) our people on spreadsheets without personal consideration. We focus on task completion, like relocating an employee or finishing an annual evaluation, ignorant of the true effect it has on a person and his or her family. We do not truly know our people, what makes them tick and how we can best lead them. We place our loyalty toward customers and investors or become consumed by our schedules and overlook — sometimes completely — our people. Countless organizations either don't invest in people well or do it at all. Some think they have it right but do not really measure the true personal impacts or effects of their efforts. Some are so focused on productivity and efficiency that they overlook the person who will help them achieve it.

Managing people using spreadsheets and automated networks is efficient and easy, although impersonal. Leading them by personally connecting with them as individuals is hard. It takes discipline and personal leadership. In the Army — where I served for 27 years — we have a great saying: *"Take the Hard Right instead of the Easy Wrong."* It was our way of highlighting that the path to the right approach usually incurs hardship while taking the wrong or lazy path is usually easy. It's time to take the *Hard Right*. There are countless people out there, each of them complex individuals who serve in public or private organizations who come to work each day seeking fulfillment. Each of these people has real passions, personal challenges, desires, personal and professional goals, and dreams — most of which go unrecognized by their supervisors. They seek counsel and development. They want to work in a disciplined environment with vision and culture, and they want to feel like they belong. They seek a lifestyle over a job. They want to be recognized for their hard work and accomplishments. They want their employers to invest in them.

Sound hard? It's really not. A little extra time and effort will go a very long way.

I wrote this book following my experience serving soldiers and their families in peacetime and combat in the United States Army. In the pages that follow, you will read about my experience investing in people as a commander or CEO of an Army Brigade of nearly 5,000 soldiers and their families. My teammates and I produced the number one brigade (of 34 brigades in total) based in the United States for human resource (HR) performance during a particularly tumultuous period. We did it through our people-centric approach. Along with this, we exceeded our soldier retention directives and goals and led our division for most of my command tenure. These are just a few of the many accomplishments we achieved. Following my retirement in 2016, I had time to reflect on my successes and failures, and connect with several leaders in the business community to see if they were taking a *personal* or *personnel* approach to investing in their people. I found several leaders and human resource professionals who took this investment seriously. Unfortunately, I found more who did not. To the champions of investing in people, I applaud your efforts. Read this book, and you will take your approach to new heights. To those who have not invested in your people, for whatever reason, please read this book. Learn from what I learned and take my approach in total or even just a small portion. I think you'll be glad you did.

I get it. You are very busy. If anyone can appreciate the demands placed on leaders at all echelons in government and private organizations, I surely can. Many jobs I held in the Army consumed me, and I had to fend off distractors that prevented me from connecting with my people. In some organizations, I succeeded; in some, I was defeated. Whether you eat the full enchilada outlined in the pages ahead, or you only take a small bite, whether you spend one hour counseling and developing a subordinate or you take 10 minutes, do something. You will see the results.

This is a book focused on leaders, either current or future. While it does have tremendous value for HR professionals, it is the leaders (in all functional areas, but especially in the C-suite or at the highest ranks), at the end of the day, who establish vision and culture, who set the tone in their organization and ultimately invest in their people in personal ways. Whether you lead a group of three people or command 30,000, come with me on a journey where I will tell some stories of my successes and failures and what I did to achieve results. While my personal experience is military, every organization consists of people, and it is our investment in them that is so important. This book and this investment transcend Army formations and tech companies, warriors and administrative assistants. It transcends gender, race, nationality, religion, etc. It leaves lofty terms and phrases, large-scale programs, or motivational speeches at the door. In the pages ahead, I will tell real stories, give you simple and practical frameworks and models that can help you. In the Army, I served a cause — the defense of my nation and the leadership and caring of America's sons and daughters and their families. Welcome to my new cause — making a difference in the lives of others by helping you invest in your people. It's *personal*, not *personnel*, so let's spend a few chapters together unpacking and understanding this thing called investing in people. Let's take the hard right instead of the easy wrong.

Chapter 1
INVESTING IN PEOPLE

I am a leader who likes to get to the root of problems, not just their symptoms, who likes to have words defined so I can fully understand the meaning and intent behind their use. Often, I say to my colleagues and family members "define that." It drives most of them nuts, but for me, it takes away the gray area or gaps in my understanding. It helps me start from a point of clarity before I offer a solution, assessment or opinion.

According to Dictonary.com, to invest is "to use, give, or devote (time, talent, etc.), as for a purpose or to achieve something." As you might invest time in a garden to take in its beauty or consume its vegetables, or as you might invest in real estate to create more income, you invest in people to gain something; that something is to make them better people. Notice I did not say increase productivity or overcome an entrenched enemy occupying a hilltop. No, the purpose behind this investment of your time, talent, etc., is to make a difference in the lives of others.

This means you invest your personal time as a leader to focus on your people by engaging with them daily, counseling (refer to Chapter 8 for my definition of counseling) and growing them and helping them to attain their goals and identify and live out their passions. You develop and manage organizational operations and processes which are people-centric, meaning they are designed and adjusted around people not with people as the afterthought. You never assume risk for caring for and investing in people. It remains a personal and organizational priority. You develop and espouse a people-centric mindset by talking about it constantly and setting a personal example. You invest time in getting to know your people and their families praising and recognizing them for their incredible feats. From this approach, finance, marketing, product development and profitability will work out. Rifle qualification, battle drill proficiency and increased physical fitness will come. It will all happen when leaders invest in people.

Entering brigade command in the 101st Airborne Division in 2013, I knew I had to focus on making people better people. I took this approach in every organization I led but never was it more critical than the fall of 2013, and I'll talk more about this when I discuss investing in people in Chapter 5. In my organization, I had numerous leaders, including myself, who could prepare us to seize a hilltop, of that I had no doubt. However, if my people were not functioning at 100 percent physically, mentally, emotionally, and spiritually none of that mattered. Moreover, if they did not feel that their leaders knew them personally and were looking out for them and their families, if they didn't understand our vision and believed in what the brigade's leadership believed in, they might not give their all to a mission to seize a hilltop or any other critical task we were sure to receive. The same is true in a business. You can study the relationship between employee activity and productivity and efficiency all day long. You can even throw in benefits like bonuses and time off, but if you do not invest in your people, as I will describe in this book, it doesn't matter. They may perform for a short period, but the effort will fail eventually.

According to the 2017 Gallup Poll, 70 percent of employees in today's workforce are not engaged at work, meaning they are not psychologically committed to their jobs, happy in the workplace and likely to be making positive contributions to their organizations. Gallup identified the causes to this disengagement as leaders and organizations who: failed to establish job expectations, listen to employee opinions, provide mission, purpose and worth, offer praise and generally show that they care for their people. Answers.com, in a study of the American worker, highlighted that more than 50 percent of employees claimed that their employer did not know if they were happy in their role, had an ongoing process to understand their job satisfaction and likelihood to stay at the company and understood what their future career goals were. This study is telling and goes on to describe the void employees are feeling about being heard, feeling engaged and having a sense of purpose in their job. For the Army, in a period of downsizing, the departure of officers and soldiers does not ring alarm bells as it might during periods of growth. However, in the magazine *The Atlantic*, a 2017 article titled "Why Our Best Officers Are Leaving," describes how the Army's best officers are departing amidst a military personnel system which rewards conformism and ignores merit. I recall times in my career when I seriously contemplated resigning. While serving as a paratrooper, my staff and I would invest so much time on the planning, rehearsing and execution of the parachute drop that once we all landed and assembled, the subsequent training event we had planned would get off to a very messy start. My boss was unsympathetic, and I bore the brunt of it. He was a boss who was never satisfied with a staff product. It took its toll on me.

Happier or "invested in" soldiers produce better results regardless of the task, this I have witnessed firsthand. Happier or "invested in" employees help companies achieve higher profits.

Jerry Dodson, the CEO of Parnassus Investments which manages the Parnassus Endeavor Fund, a top performing mutual fund, focuses its investments in companies off the *Fortune Magazine*'s Top 100 Companies to Work For list. Dodson posits that elements that define a good workplace, from benefits like health insurance and childcare to cultural collegiality, advancement opportunities, and faith in management are linked to meaningful qualities that drive up stock prices, such as talent retention (leading to lower turnover costs) and increased productivity. "If you take good care of your employees, if you treat them well, if you pay them fairly, they're going to work harder," Dodson says, "If you don't, there are many ways that they can sabotage your business."

If investing in people is as important as these well-known studies reveal, then why are leaders failing? Moreover, what are the root causes of this? There are several, and I'll take these on in the pages ahead. To summarize, these causes consist of: avoidance of confrontation, leaders uncomfortable, uneducated, untrained or unwilling to counsel and develop people, demanding organizational and personal schedules, failure to see the tangible effects of investing, lack of self-awareness and introspection, a focus on or confusion over management versus leadership, and a loyalty to impersonal terms and process over person.

THE "I'M TOO BUSY" MYTH

Military and private businesses seem to be busier now than at any time in history. Debatably, some of it is self-inflicted as leaders plow through mounds of data, tackle the crisis of the moment or fall victim to all their electronic gadgets. I know from my Army experience, our "can do" attitude would sure lead to a full calendar and daily schedule. I worked insane hours in many of my jobs just because the task list was greater than hours in the day. A Harvard Business School survey of 1,000 professionals found that 94 percent worked at least 50 hours a week and almost half worked more than 65 hours. Ever-improving and efficient "time saving" devices like smartphones and web conferencing programs now allow people to conduct work far beyond the office and well outside the nine to five work day. Whether it's self-inflicted or task overload something has to give. That something is usually people.

I have a special appreciation for this, having served as a commander of several large organizations. It took a lot of my time to write counseling statements and efficiency reports and counsel my leaders in person. My time walking around talking to my soldiers and their families came at a cost of other demands placed on me internally or by my higher headquarters. Business leaders, with all the demands placed on them, especially with small or non-existent supporting staffs are so consumed by running their business daily that they see right past the needs of their people and opportunities to invest in them. I don't buy the argument that "I'm too busy." Reflecting back on numerous assignments I could have and should have made the time to invest in my subordinates. I remembered the event I was focused on instead of the person I should have been, and it was the person who deserved the attention more than the task. It required setting and sticking to priorities and the management of my own personal task list. In Chapter 5 you will read about how I overcame this amidst a very busy organizational and personal schedule. I get the personal task load argument, and though there were days when the schedule conquered me, there were more when I conquered it and made a difference in the life of another person and his or her family. The results were amazing.

I believe if we connect with people, truly know them and become the champion of their passions and goals, we can have a profound positive impact on them. If we do the hard work to overcome our schedules, fears, lack of training, etc., our organizations will soar. Our people will break through brick walls for us and their teammates. They'll conduct themselves ethically and in the best interests of the organization. They'll be better soldiers, drivers, salesman and educators. They'll be better husbands, wives and citizens in their community. They'll be better people.

Chapter 2
AN IMPERSONAL APPROACH TO A PERSONAL ENDEAVOR

Impersonal means you think or act without consideration for persons or personal feelings. You are influenced by and act upon things that do not include people. I do believe that leaders wake each morning wanting to do well by their organization and persons around them. There are exceptions, but I am an optimist and approach all people from a position of trust, believing they want to do right. Amidst all this, we still have people who are unfulfilled and disengaged in the workplace. We should not ignore the data or believe we have it completely right in our organizations. I certainly didn't in mine. Taking on the causes that take our attention away from people, in this chapter I will examine two: impersonal titles and terms, and impersonal processes. I'll also give my assessment of our human resource (HR) professionals or our ambassadors of this investment and the departments in which they serve.

IMPERSONAL TITLES, TERMS, AND PROCESSES

Impersonal titles and terms. Words do not themselves treat people poorly, leaders do, and these lofty words and phrases and their associated processes cloud over the reality and need of human connection and contribute to the problem. Along with my experiences in the Army, in my research for this book, I spoke to more than 75 business leaders and HR professionals. In most of those conversations, I rarely heard the word "people." I felt as if we were talking about the management of machines instead of the leadership and care of people. "Human" was used but only in conjunction with another word like "human resources" or "human capital." Instead, I was bombarded with words and phrases such as labor productivity equations, employee interface, performance management, predictive human productivity index and relationship management to name a few. Some even used these terms with pride as if to showcase their expertise. I felt like I was conversing with R2D2 from *Star Wars*. I'd consider these words innocent victims if I had not experienced and witnessed the impersonal treatment of people and their families in some military units and places of employment.

Comedian George Carlin did a piece on euphemisms several years ago where he amusingly describes the softening of words and language to strip away their harsh core meaning. In the piece, he describes how "shell shock," the powerful term used in World War I to describe mental trauma brought on by violent combat experience evolved into "battle fatigue" then finally to "post-traumatic stress disorder" (PTSD). He described how the terror associated with shell shock was lost deep inside a softer, easier stated PTSD and how if shell shock was still used during the Vietnam era, veterans might have received better treatment. It's hard to prove that a word or phrase resulted in the lack of proper treatment for combat veterans (though their lack of treatment is a fact) but there is clear evidence of the evolution of professional language over the years from hard short terms to softer multi-word terms which cloud over their true meaning. Carlin goes on to describe this: the dump became the landfill, toilet paper became bathroom tissue, hospitals became health maintenance organizations or wellness centers, used cars became pre-owned vehicles, and the list went on. Save for the seriousness of PTSD; the comedy routine is funny yet telling. Many words and terms and their associated processes used in leading people have suffered the same fate. Even I, a seasoned leader, have to stop and think about what employee interface and relationship management means. Because of this, my focus is taken off people and placed on the processes I think these terms represent.

Let's start with the two most frequently used titles, human resources (HR) and human capital (HC). HR sounds like a basket of humans like a bushel of apples where we pick out the best one, consume it and get on with our lives. A resource as defined by Macmillan dictionary is "something that you can use to help you to achieve something, especially in your work or study." How about Human Capital? This one sounds like a storage room full of people unhooked from their power sources wearing tags displaying how much profit they can produce. Make sure you pick the one with the highest productivity label! Neither term exists without controversy. Human resource was first used in the early 1900s and depicted workers as capital assets. Economist E. Wight Bakke, credited for modernizing the term, used it in a report in 1958 where he described human resource as a function in a company with specific management tasks rather than a focus on human behaviors and relationships. Professionals in labor and academia criticized the term claiming that human beings are not "commodities" or "resources," but are creative and social beings in a productive enterprise. In 2004, "human capital" was named the German Un-Word of the Year by a jury of scholars who considered the term inappropriate and inhumane, as individuals would be degraded and their abilities classified according to economically relevant quantities.

I don't know about you, but I would rather not be referred to as a resource. I realize that an organization is going to *use* my skills, experience, training and personal drive like it would energy to run its machines or parts to build its products. That's okay, but the difference is we often treat people as we would energy or parts; we squeeze every bit out of them, cast them aside and expect they will be back the next day for more. Human capital is a term I would not prefer either. Capital has a worse connotation than resource. It gives off more of an ownership sentiment. You might nurture a resource knowing you will want it in its best form when you need it next. Capital just gets used and forgotten. I've seen some organizations use terms like team member, executive, associate or specialist. In the military, we are soldiers, sailors, airmen, marines or coast guardsmen. These certainly have a better ring to them. I think of people when I hear them; I do not think of people when I hear resource or capital.

In the Vietnam War, service members used the derogatory term "Gook" to describe their Asian adversaries and people of the region. This word, which contributed to the dehumanization of a people, led some soldiers and units to the barbaric treatment of both enemy combatants and innocent civilians on the battlefield. The same happened in Iraq and Afghanistan with the acts of some individuals and units urinating on deceased enemy bodies and collecting body parts. These acts were the exception, not the norm as a vast majority of individuals and units overcame this stigma and conducted themselves honorably. Yet they seemed to receive all the attention and lead to a perceived widespread behavior which was problematic. David Livingstone Smith, in his book *Less Than Human*, states, "When people dehumanize others, they actually conceive of them as subhuman creatures." I do not for a minute imagine any leader going to the extreme of barbarism in the workplace, but the comparison is important. The more we dehumanize titles, terms and processes the less we see the humans affected by them. People want to be referred to and treated as people. Maybe in the workplace if Mary was referred to and thought of as Mary the generous, dedicated person with a great sense of humor who just bought a condo and got engaged last month instead of "employee 0037 the Audio Visual Technician" or if Army Private Atkinson was known as Bob Atkinson from Philly with an expensive sports car and a one-year-old son who is working through a divorce from his wife instead of "Atkinson the rifleman who can run a mile in 6:24," we might view them as people instead of resources or *capital*.

Now I know the publishing of this book does not mean the end to terms and processes like labor productivity equations and work-force solutions. Additionally, I do not predict the Society for Human Resource Management (SHRM) changes its name to the Society for Investing in People (SIP) although it would be a refreshing change, in my opinion. One positive trend worth noting is the hiring of a Chief People Officer (CHPO) instead of a Chief HR Officer (CHRO) in organizations. This certainly is a sign that some leaders recognize the importance of titles and see HR as too old-fashioned for the modern workplace. Even under traditional titles, there is still room on this earth and a dire need for good HR professionals (who are people, too!). It is how we conduct ourselves and lead our organizations and people and how we humanize our processes that are most important. I commanded a large organization that used all these terms. We managed personnel readiness using AHRS and EMILPO which stood for Army Human Resource System and Electronic Military Personnel Office respectively. These systems existed to help the Army determine if units were ready to deploy to combat on short notice. They didn't have a function that took into account Private Atkinson's family and financial situation. I was not going to let these terms and processes prevent my leaders and me from connecting with our people. I had rock stars who managed my soldiers using AHRS and EMILPO, and they were the best in the Army. I was blessed to have them. I stayed focused on the human being. Where I could "humanize" these systems and where I could change terms and titles, I would. I never lost sight of the person behind "employee 0037." To some, this would be a human resource or capital on a spreadsheet. To me, it was a human being with a story. I wanted to know who it was, get to know them and help them be the best they could be. I talked about this personal approach every day in my organization in an effort to get my teammates to think about it like I did.

Impersonal processes. Some organizational processes do serve a purpose however many are too process-centric as if managing a fleet of forklifts instead of people-centric. I'll cover in detail the dreaded personnel data sheet later in the book which is one example. Here I'll use employee performance evaluations to illustrate my point. As a process, I have seen a variety of approaches to evaluating people; never done, done as a continuous process through an organizational social website or done annually in an efficiency report. Some organizations use a combination of these. For the ones who choose not to do it all, there is one guarantee; their employees are walking around clueless as to whether they are performing well, if they measure up to their peers or if they have potential for advancement. It's difficult if not impossible to grow or discipline a person if you fail to give them feedback on their performance. If they possess bad habits or require development to perform their job better, it might never be discovered let alone occur.

For annual performance evaluations, business analysts and consultants have debated over their utility. Many see them as an impersonal "check the block" form which needs to be completed regardless of their value to the employee. The emphasis on many of these annual appraisals is on form completion instead of the growth and development of a person. Moreover, many professionals question how a supervisor can effectively assess a full year of performance on one form and in one setting. According to CEB Global (now Gartner) a business advisory firm, only four percent of HR managers say their system of assessing employees is effective. Some leaders have listened to HR and their people and are moving away from year-end appraisals as well as employee rank-ordering as they see little value in it. Jack Welch, the former CEO of General Electric, made famous the "Rank and Yank" method of rank-ordering his best workers and firing those in the bottom percentages. In some organizations, this annual evaluation is being replaced by processes designed to give more continuous feedback and grow employees.

Many of these web-based feedback systems enable peer comments following employee performances like briefings, product design, etc. Numerous companies are now offering employee performance or feedback software to streamline and modernize current processes. The problem with most of these programs is that they do not require in-person delivery. Most are shared sites where an employee can answer survey questions, provide his or her own analysis of performance or view feedback from peers and supervisors in chat-box or email form. Supervisors can access information on their people and produce their assessment yet there is no forcing function to require person-to-person connection.

Digital communication, while convenient and common place with smartphones and business networks is the worst for personal dialogue and conflict resolution. Shirley Engelmeier, CEO of InclusionINC, a global consulting firm states "Digital communications seem efficient but, when aggregated over time, create an 'Ethernet' wall that makes office life less personal, less human, less engaging and eventually less fulfilling." If the evaluation is personal it should include an individual's personal and professional positives and negatives. Through the use of these programs much can be lost and misinterpreted from a performance graph or sentence or phrase typed in a text box. In digital communication, there is no requirement to respond to feedback as there would be in personal communication. There is no back and forth dialogue so critical to development. Text comments like "You should keep your hands down by your side when you conduct presentations," or "Your proposal was very good but a bit lengthy" are what I call "vanilla" or marginally helpful to properly evaluate and grow a person. A one-on-one conversation about the deficiencies a person possesses which causes him or her to be too animated when speaking or too wordy when creating written correspondence and how to overcome them would serve the person far better. There is great value in many of these web-based programs, and I vote for effective constant or periodic feedback over nothing at all but while leaders achieve efficiency they put at risk vital human connection.

Most government organizations still use the annual performance evaluation to assess their people. For Army officers, we used the Officer Evaluation Report (OER). This annual evaluation is designed to be complemented by a support form used to outline an officer's duties and responsibilities and objectives for the year ahead. The support form, intended to be a living document, could be updated by an officer and his rater with objectives and accomplishments as the rating period progressed. The form and the evaluation process were designed to facilitate interaction between the rated officer and his or her superior. Unfortunately, few if any are held to this standard. The support form was usually done in haste once the OER came due. My rater and I had to look back 12 months to recall events which described my performance. That was always a challenge. Like most officers, I was rarely counseled, so the contents of the OER usually came as a surprise. The OER became so inflated in the Army that any negative comment on the form was the kiss of death. Choice of words on the form became a form of art. Raters used a hierarchy of words to communicate to promotion boards. Words and phrases like *outstanding* or *solid performance* or *great officer* would be translated as *marginal performer*. The form did have a ranking section where an officer could be grouped (above center, center, below) amongst peers in his organization. Senior raters (officers had raters and senior raters evaluating them) were held to percentages (49 percent in above center ratings) to prevent them from handing everyone top ratings. The Army took great strides to hold senior raters accountable for managing percentages but did little to enforce one-on-one counseling.

Many organizations who still use the annual appraisal or evaluation form without continuous personal feedback and development, do not serve their people well. They are forced to capture a year's worth of performance on one form. Identifying deficiencies at the end of the year is too late. Leaders do not wait until year's end to fix machines that are deficient. They address machine deficiencies when they learn of them. We should take the same approach with our people. Annual evaluations like the OER, if done right, should be more of a year-end formality instead of a discovery of things not addressed or not known. If the rater had done his or her job with periodic one-on-one counseling which identified and addressed strengths and weak-nesses, then the OER or the annual performance evaluation should be a simple form to fill out. The evaluation should be a growing workable document as the year progresses. At a minimum, there should be no surprises come evaluation time if the leader has taken a personal approach to the process. Remember Ken's experience I shared in the introduction? In the alternative approach, Ken and his supervisor quickly reviewed his annual evaluation because they had spent personal time together discussing his performance over the year. Ken walked into the one-on-one session already knowing what to expect.

There are advantages and disadvantages to the employee evaluation process whichever one you choose. I'm less concerned with the type than I am with the leader's approach to connecting with his or her subordinates in a personal way. Agnostic of the process, it's leaders who choose to provide feedback and assessments in person or not. I didn't fault the Army for not enforcing a progressive counseling program to complement the OER. I failed to do it a few times early in my career. In one situation, I had a subordinate who I believed was under-performing and I wanted to communicate that to the Army review board via his annual efficiency report. However, I failed to conduct periodic counseling on paper to document his failures, direct corrective action, and measure improvement. I had a few conversations with him where I would verbalize his failures, but I didn't document it. I believed he understood my assessment of him through our conversations but when I completed his annual report he was surprised, and he protested. Out of fairness, I adjusted his report only slightly, but I learned a great lesson from this. He was right to be surprised and right to protest. I was wrong for not investing time communicating his shortfalls formally, on paper and challenging him to improve. I wouldn't make this mistake again. However you decide to conduct evaluations in this personal journey, remember to find a way to connect in person formally. Document it but most importantly, make it personal.

THE FEW, THE HATED, THE HR DEPARTMENT

In my personal experience and research, I found one commonality; everyone hates HR. Think about it, is anyone really excited to head over to the HR department? I haven't found anyone. It sounds like a prison sentence. "You've been sentenced to spend the night in the HR Department!" It's a department where people are pushed onto an assembly line belt, run through a few machines which beat you up, spit you out onto subsequent belts then finally drop you off into a segregated box where you are filed neatly, next to all the other human resources like a box of Christmas tree ornaments, stored away until your human capital is needed. Scott Adams, the artist of the *Dilbert* comic strip, created Catbert, the Evil Director of Human Resources and used this character in numerous cartoon sketches poking fun at HR and HR directors. Along with Dilbert himself, the impersonal boss and his impersonal approaches, the Catbert cartoons are funny, yet they illustrate the disdain shared widely in the business and government community of HR. There has been much written about its causes. Liz Ryan, a former corporate executive and *Forbes Magazine* contributor, does an effective job at highlighting this in an article titled "Ten Reasons Everyone Hates HR." She points out one cause as being poorly selected HR employees who understand policies but little about the company. She goes on, "Some of these HR employees buried deep inside HR departments far away from the organization's population have trouble seeing the 'human side' of any issue and focus instead on keeping every process uniform and exception-free." Keith H. Hammonds of *Fast Company* attributes lack of strategic vision and a seat at the CEO's table and too much outsourcing as causal to this hatred in his 2005 article "Why We Hate HR."

Like the term Human Resources, the organizations and organizational approach it represents has its controversial roots. HR has its founding with Elton Mayo's 1930's Human Relations Movement that examined the effects of social relations, motivation and employee satisfaction in the workplace as a way to achieve economic efficiency.

Conversely, E. Wight Bakke claimed in his 1958 publication, *The Human Resources Function*, that productive work and efficiency and not personal happiness was the function of HR. Moreover, contrast Mayo's movement with Fredrick Taylor's Scientific Management approach dubbed "Taylorism," which centered on economic efficiency. Taylorism was criticized as being man-contemptuous, turning the worker into automation or a machine.

To be fair, I know there are countless people who work in progressive human resource organizations who do actually care about the people they serve and see them as an investment rather than a cost. Of the good ones, I found they were all characterized by the following three attributes:

1. They had very outgoing people in them who came across as quite engaged and interested in how they could help solve a person's problem. This was indicative of hiring processes to place the right people in HR.

2. They incorporated better environments (or worked with their boss to do so) such as providing fitness facilities and adjusting work spaces and hours to allow people to have work-life balance.

3. They relied on better employee feedback systems and processes. While many were void of person-to-person connection requirements, in the good HR organizations, I witnessed continuous feedback systems and two-way feedback processes that resulted in employees better aware of their performance and standing and leaders who had a clearer view of the positive and negative effects of their leadership.

To these organizations, I applaud their authentic approach to HR and apologize for batching them in with others that don't. I always remember trying to find the one or two people in my unit's personnel section who I knew were genuinely dedicated to helping. Unfortunately, it's the few bad apples in these departments (which have no business being there) that ruin it for the good ones. Furthermore, it is the perception of disservice which cannot be overlooked. If disservice is perceived, then it is real. Consumers (and employees) vote with their feet and take their business elsewhere when they experience disservice. Business leaders place enormous emphasis on preventing customer disservice, yet many ignore this when it comes to their own employees. Would you return to a restaurant or car repair shop if you were treated poorly? Probably not. Your bad experience might have been an exception in an otherwise highly-regarded business but to you that does not matter. You won't risk returning. Have you ever had an experience like this in the HR department? In our organizations, we are stuck with these departments no matter how big or small they are. If you experience a restaurant or repair shop-like experience in HR, your choice may be to avoid the place at all costs or enter with a chip on your shoulder ready to do battle.

Certainly, most people understand this is not a one-way street and to be fair, in many cases, employees are to blame for their own misunderstandings or even misbehavior. Most people understand there are organizational needs which may outweigh their own. They understand the big picture and know that personnel management requirements, though burdensome, are necessary. I may have balked at some of the forms I had to fill out in my HR experiences, but I knew, for the most part, many of them were required. It's the poor delivery of personnel services and treatment of employees amongst other reasons previously mentioned which gives the HR department a bad name. People take it personally and they should. This oversight does not bode well for any organization which relies on its people, and it's not the relationship any organization desires between its employees and its HR department. This is a leadership problem, not just an HR manager's problem. HR managers work for business or military leaders who are charged with investing in their people. Leaders who wish to have a healthy, personal work environment should give their HR manager a seat at the table and see him or her often. I'll speak more to this later in the book but remember this and consider it in your organization. Poll your people and learn their perception.

It is time we put the *human* back into human resources. I have seen words like "people" included in official titles like the CHPO and "culture" included into processes which are certainly a step in the right direction. Imagine walking into the "People First Department" (or another welcoming title) greeted by a friendly individual who actively listens to your concerns and takes visible, concrete steps to help you. Think of an HR professional who asks about your family situation and is prepared to offer help or include your family considerations into your personnel file or personnel action. Better yet, think about an HR professional who already knows that your child is about to enter their high school senior year or first year in college or that your spouse is due to give birth soon. Think about an HR professional who discovers a training course coming up and notifies your supervisor because he or she knows you need it to advance in the company. These departments might be a better place to walk into. People might actually enjoy paying frequent visits to the "People First Department."

THE US ARMY'S IMPERSONAL BEHEMOTH, PERSONNEL COMMAND

When I first entered the Army in 1990, US Army Personnel Command or PERSCOM managed all the Army's people. Their functions, among many, included efficiency reports, certifications, and unit assignments. There was nothing wrong with the title PERSCOM but it's the reputation it developed that contributed to the Army's decision to change it. PERSCOM became a four-letter word representing everything not related to investing in people. "PERSCOM," mentioned in Army social circles symbolized this behemoth of an organization which existed just to screw with you. We all envisioned PERSCOM employees each morning in their Catbert pajamas enjoying their coffee plotting their next move against us. One of PERSCOM's most important functions was determining our next assignment likely to take us to an entirely different state or country. You could submit a preference sheet which outlined your assignment preferences, but these sheets seemed to vanish into the PERSCOM black hole with little to no consideration. You might learn of your next assignment through the mail or from some impersonal assignment officer only concerned with accomplishing the task of assigning you to your next duty station. This might even happen without warning or consult. In 2003, PERSCOM became Army Human Resource Command or HRC. This change centered on combining Army Reserve with the active Army to gain some efficiencies. Along with its new name came a better approach to connecting with soldiers. We saw more frequent visits to Army installations from the different departments across HRC and the Army did make strides addressing an over-inflated OER system. However, some of the same people and processes from the PERSCOM days remained in the building.

I recall a friend of mine receiving an email from his HRC manager stating he had selected his next assignment and it was a great one but that he needed to call to learn what it was. As it turns out, it was an assignment to Fort Polk, Louisiana. Nothing against the great state of Louisiana, but this location was on the bottom of most officers' preference sheets. I was stationed there, so I can personally attest. I knew very few people who desired to be stationed at Fort Polk. It was a long distance from big cities, and the schools were not the greatest. In fairness, the Army did need quality officers there because it was one of three Army combat training centers that trained and evaluated units in preparation for combat deployments. Many officers had passed through the gates of Fort Polk on to very successful careers.

HRC personnel managers knew this assignment would be met with resistance. Using email to notify a soldier of an assignment to Fort Polk was a bad option. This assignment required a personal conversation and because it was such an undesirable location perhaps an incentive for accepting it. Assignments to Korea, when I first entered the Army, were unaccompanied, meaning family members could not accompany their service member and had to remain in the United States (this later changed.) The assignments were only one year in length due to family separation and soldiers were offered an assignment of choice following their tour. HRC might have offered the same to my friend following his tour at Fort Polk or explained the career benefits of duty at Fort Polk. There were career benefits to serving there which might have changed the outlook for my friend and others in the same predicament. Whatever the outcome, this assignment required a personal conversation, not a "send-and-forget" email. This is an important vignette and one of my central reasons for writing this book. This machine-like approach to a directive changing someone's life required a personal approach, not a personnel approach.

As a soldier, the Army was going to move you frequently even to places you did not particularly enjoy. I moved 16 times in 27 years and knew that was part of the profession. My family and I enjoyed each new adventure. Those who were opposed to frequent moves left the service for a new career and lifestyle. My issue and that of many soldiers was not the frequent moves or duty in places like Fort Polk but rather the process by which you were given orders taking you to a new location. The Army provided very good money compensation to support the move of soldiers and their families as well as ample time for travel and vacation if desired. However, the process was done largely agnostic of a soldier's personal situation.

Here is a scenario which, unfortunately, occurs frequently. I'll use Drew, a fictional soldier, for this example. Drew receives orders from HRC directing a no-later-than arrival date to his new duty station of February 20th. Drew has a wife and two children. His orders come via email on the 18th of December. On the surface, all looks clean to an assignment officer. Drew has his orders; the Army gets to fill a vacancy in another unit, task complete. However, there's something big missing. Drew's wife works full-time. He purchased a home for his family and is paying on a mortgage. His daughters are both in high school. The oldest is in her senior year. This clean scenario just got very messy. To HRC, it was a personnel move achieving *personnel* management. To Drew and his family, it's *personal* achieving inconvenience and family strife. Either Drew will have to uproot his family and take them along or depart on his own and leave his wife and children behind only to join him when his girls finish school, his oldest graduates and his wife can transition out of her job and either sell or rent the house. Consider the hardship placed upon this family due to a simple set of orders directing a February move delivered by email without family consideration. Drew can ask for an extension or cancellation of his orders, but he is unlikely to see any significant changes. If his HRC assignment officer had known and considered this, he could have done some extra work to either find another available soldier matching Drew's qualifications or work on delaying Drew's move until after his daughter graduates. There are usually options that might facilitate a smoother transition for Drew. They may burden the personnel system a bit as the Army works to put the right soldier in the right place at the right time. However, in this case, the burden is instantly off the back of the Army and placed on Drew and his family. What condition will Drew be in when he arrives at this new duty station, especially if he has left his family behind? Perhaps if the Army could have waited until May, Drew and his family could have prepared, and he could have been present to watch his daughter graduate.

In my 27-year Army career, my fellow soldiers and I experienced this hardship in some (not all) of our assignments. Like good soldiers, we accepted orders to new installations, packed our bags, prepared our families and pulled children from school and spouses from jobs to meet the Army's needs. Some put up a fight, but few won. Like the HR departments in businesses, not all who served in HRC were of ill-will. Many in fact, were selfless servers trying to do right by the individual and his or her family. They just seemed to be in bad company, or it was the few who spoiled it for the many good. HRC continued to assign officers and enlisted soldiers in very impersonal ways. Because of this, HRC is not a place that many soldiers want to communicate with or serve. Few want to talk to HRC on a reoccurring basis, and many have personal stories which do not reflect well on the organization. This, I know, is not the relationship the Army wants between its soldiers and the organization which manages them. I departed the Army enormously grateful for every assignment. I, like so many other soldiers, knew the Army needed us where and when it needed us, especially in a time of war. I just wish the conversation and understanding between the soldier and his or her personnel manager and the processes by which the Army managed its people could have been better. How is this process similar to processes in your organization?

GETTING PERSONAL

Now that I have slung mud on the HR community and the Army, some of you are probably ready to set fire to this book in a public place. Some of you are probably cheering. I could fill pages full of great products and processes being used by leaders and HR professionals in business and the Army. I could relate stories of CEOs and military commanders who connected with their people and made a positive difference like the CEO who helped an employee achieve an unfulfilled dream or a commander who made a personal call to delay the move of a soldier due to his spouse about to give birth. I could show examples of HR professionals who cut through impersonal words and processes, but then I wouldn't really contribute much other than praise. I highlight these examples among many which illustrate that many organizations are missing the human-to-human connection, that while they may not intend so, their products and procedures are not conducive to investing in people.

WHAT YOU CAN DO

Here is a checklist you can use to overcome the challenges I have mentioned in this chapter.

- Ban or change terms and titles
- Establish organizational people-centric policies or regulations
- Set a personal example in word and deed
- Work to change the mindset of your people
- Establish an HR vision
- Hire the right people
- Train and develop HR members

- Conduct a grand re-opening for your HR department
- Measure the effects of these changes (refer to Chapter 9)

Ban or change terms and titles that are causal to impersonal approaches in your organization. If it sounds "personnel" and not "personal" or if you cannot envision a person when saying it, change it. Do it formally through an organizational policy and announcement, so everyone understands. Be the first and most frequent member to use people-centric terms such as the "People First Department." Change the mindset of your leaders and HR department through your personal leadership and communication. Never review an HR change or initiative without inquiring about its effect on people. Never look at a personnel process without questioning its purpose or finding a way to make it more human. In your HR department, no matter how big or small, create a vision. Ensure it is a shared vision among HR members and/or employees. Choose the right HR professionals to help you write it. Envision a variety of experiences from the lens of a person in your organization. Ensure all products, procedures, official terms and phrases reflect what is espoused in the vision statement and ensure it is nested with the larger organization's vision. Change the name of your HR department to something more appropriate and welcoming. Establish a comprehensive interview process for new HR hires and a training program for existing members to ensure they are prepared to deliver. Employ caring, committed professionals. Once you have all the new procedures set and training complete, rename the HR department and conduct a grand re-opening. It must look and feel different to your employees. If you have to outsource HR functions, be personally involved with this outsourcing to ensure those who conduct HR functions understand your people-centric intent. Most importantly, measure the effect of this rebirth using employee interviews and short surveys.

This change, if done right, would have immeasurable impact on the most important portion of your organization, its people.

Visit *www.RobCampbellLeadership.com/Book* for additional material on making improvements to your HR department.

Chapter 3
MACHINES AND WEBSITES ARE IMPORTANT; PEOPLE ARE INDISPENSABLE

WHY PEOPLE ARE IMPORTANT

We live in an incredibly fast-paced interconnected world. In business as on the battlefield, the actions of one employee or soldier can have strategic impact. Within minutes their actions, inactions or misconduct can make national headlines or spread like wildfire in social networks. People are central to all that we do. They hold all the keys to success and failure in our organizations. They stand at the point of execution of our directives, values, and vision. They answer our phones, reply to our customers, drive our company-labeled vehicles, sell our products, detain our prisoners of war, and care for our soldiers, employees and their families. They can be our champions or the ones who ruin us and our organizations. They are enormously important yet, in many ways, we fail to understand this. Leaders fail to promote environments which accommodate the desires of our people resulting in disengagement.

To demonstrate the importance of people in my own organization, I used an important comparison. In a small 30-man Army organization called the infantry platoon, automatic machine guns are assigned as organic weapons. This is the key weapon for a small infantry unit, the one which could change the course of a firefight against a committed foe. Lives depended on them. Every week we faithfully operated and maintained these weapons to become intimately familiar with them and to ensure their proper function. We fired them often under myriad conditions, and when one of these weapons malfunctioned, people went to work on it immediately. The weapon would only be placed back in secure storage after it was cleaned and functioning flawlessly. We relied upon these weapons to be at their best because we might deploy anywhere in the world literally overnight. Soldiers would go to any extreme to ensure our machine guns were perfect even if it meant staying at work all night. I didn't need to say or do much to emphasize the importance of investing in these weapons. It was like instructing everyone to breathe oxygen. Every soldier and leader knew it had to be done. It was in our DNA. Once I described this to my team, I could then stress the importance of our people who we would rely on as we would our machine guns. We would place even greater reliance on our people. Once they understood this, I could go to work battling bad titles, terms and processes and other problems and their causes challenging everyone to think and act in a people-centric way.

Practically every organization has something similar to a machine gun. It might be its website or a machine that produces its products. Because of their importance, employees would go to the same extremes to ensure they functioned without flaw. Consider an e-commerce business and how its employees must be intimately familiar with its web page. These employees would come to the immediate aid of a malfunctioning web page regardless of the time of day because the business and livelihoods depended on it. A few bad moments on the web page and the business could risk survival as customers would go elsewhere. Wouldn't we consider a rifleman or an infantry company commander just as important as a machine gun or website? Wouldn't we consider our lead engineer, or HR manager the same way? Most would answer yes. If this is so, then we should take the same approach to caring for and investing in them. We should know them as well as we do our weapons and websites. We should invest the time in helping them operate at 100 percent before we let them leave for the day. We want them to be as committed and dedicated as us, and we cannot be with them at every turn to ensure they are. They will not adopt our level of commitment and motivation automatically. We have to work at this. One key is to understand what they desire. It is a personal journey we as leaders must take so that we do not lose the customer we so desperately needed or we do not create irreparable damage to a reputation gained by the blood, sweat and tears of those who went before. It's a personal journey to make people better people.

Consider the actions of a few immoral and undisciplined soldiers in the prison of Abu Ghraib in Iraq in 2003. Abu Ghraib, an Iraqi prison under Saddam Hussein was captured by US forces following the 2003 invasion. It became the site of prisoner torture and abuses at the hands of a small group of corrupt American soldiers. Evidence, including photographs of obscene poses and torturous techniques against Iraqi prisoners, surfaced as a result of media and International Red Cross discoveries resulting in a Congressional investigation. Following the initial invasion and the fall of Baghdad, major hostilities subsided in the late spring of 2003 as the United States attempted to stabilize the country following years of oppressive rule. Post-invasion Iraq was a bleeding wound, and its success or failure rested on the shoulders of people in uniform. We all know the violence that would follow this period, but following the seizure of Baghdad and ousting of Saddam's government, the country was fractured, wounded and in need of stabilization. It was a period of opportunity. The Iraqi citizenry and the greater Middle East were watching intently the behavior and reaction of the United States in this Muslim nation. The actions of these soldiers had strategic impact, and military and political leaders rushed to condemn them and explain to a greater Middle East that this was not the intent of the Americans in Iraq. The impact of the events and the photos that went public are still being felt today. Some argue it may have set us back permanently in our efforts in the region.

Upon my retirement from the Army, my family and I were trying to decide whether to rent or buy a home by the beach in North Carolina where we wanted to start the next chapter of our lives. I did not have a follow-on job yet, so I set about trying to explore less permanent options. I called a real estate agency one day to ask about long-term and short-term home rentals. I wasn't looking for a weekly vacation rental. Our plan was a short-term rental then eventual homeownership. After explaining my situation to the person at the agency, she was very negative and condescending as if I had inconvenienced her. Of course, I was asking for something a bit out of the ordinary, but I wanted to do business with them. Moreover, I had longer term plans to do some investing in rental properties, so I was seeking a long-term relationship. They did not know it, but I was testing their organization with this phone call. Needless to say, this company did not receive any future business referrals from me.

Consider the importance of people given these two vignettes. No good leader would ever direct prisoner or customer maltreatment. It was never the intent of the United States Army to torture prisoners and commit immoral acts such as those that happened in Abu Ghraib. That's counter to the Army's core values and everything we were taught as soldiers. I know the owner of the real estate company I called would love to have my business. If it were he or she I had spoken with, I am sure they would have done everything to satisfy my needs and earn my business. If the senior leaders were present in that prison, those acts would never have happened or would have been stopped immediately, and the soldiers punished.

Now imagine these two vignettes under engaged leaders who invested in their people. The soldiers representing their nation who committed those heinous acts might have been discovered through a formal counseling program where their supervisor learned more about them, their background, their values, personal beliefs and how they saw their role managing prisoners of war. These leaders might have caught behaviors or thoughts that led to the atrocities which occurred. Maybe if the owner or the supervisor of the real estate agency I wanted to do business with had invested in his or her employee, she might have gone the extra mile to help me. Her positive, helpful approach would have produced a loyal customer instead of the opposite. Maybe if the leaders in both organizations were engaged and knew that these people were not operating at their peak, they could have prevented them from conducting their duties.

Unfortunately, leadership voids like these are common. If it's not conducting customer service or treating prisoners of war humanely, it could be the energy (or lack thereof) an employee gives when trying to earn business for his or her company. It could be the compulsion of an employee to report fraudulent behavior in the organization placing themselves at risk amongst the perpetrator(s) and other members. Cold call a company you believe should possess some very good customer service and test out this theory. Present scenarios like these or create ones to share with your subordinates to demonstrate the importance of people. See how they would react. If the answer is not what you would like, look yourself in the mirror and ask why that is the case.

DESIRES OF OUR PEOPLE

What do people really desire? How can we lead organizations that best cater to their needs? If we are to invest in our people, then this question is an important one. You can tackle impersonal terms and processes or disservice in your HR department to the delight of your people but, leaders must answer this question formally if we are to succeed. The answer will obviously vary from person to person. I had more than 70 different subordinate organizational leaders serving under me in my two-year tenure in brigade command, each with different desires. Some needed more autonomy than others. Some required more praise and recognition and others more professional growth.

If you research desires of people, specifically soldiers and employees, you will encounter, as I did, myriad lists and theories. They all have value and if implemented would have a big impact on your people. Indeed, the whole study of human psychology would serve any leader well, but I, along with many in leadership positions, do not have that educational benefit. Maslow's Hierarchy of Needs, being the most prominent theory, is a great start. Successful organizations that thrive in caring for their people have given this theory study and implementation. Jim Hughes, a lifestyle coach for Olympic athletes, business executives and military officers uses Maslow's Hierarchy to describe the evolution of employment and pursuit of purpose and fulfillment in the workplace. Jim highlights how the workforce, who once only sought to work for basic needs like food, water, etc., now seeks more of the five needs Maslow includes in his pyramid such as esteem and self-actualization. The workforce is seeking a lifestyle over a job. I used Maslow's theory as a foundation and resource when thinking about and developing the framework I would use as a leader, though I wanted to streamline it down to simple words and concepts which I thought best covered the desires of most people. Moreover, though, I wanted to emphasize fulfillment in my own theory, I knew that some desires would need primacy over others, so I didn't want to box myself in with a hierarchy as Maslow did.

Because I took investing in people so seriously, I needed to create a desires template I could bring with me into a wide variety of environments and organizations. This template or list would be my start point from which I could shift or emphasize one desire over another as required. I would use this list starting at the organizational level to examine if I was creating an environment that catered to my people. If I didn't like what I discovered, I could alter my leadership approach, change our operational procedures or conduct education and training to name a few. To develop my list, I reflected on the leaders I had worked for and the climates they established, both good and bad. I reflected on what I desired as a subordinate. I recalled environments from peacetime and war where I was charged with preparing men and women for combat and remembered what they desired to be at their very best. Lastly, my tours in Afghanistan greatly informed and shaped my theory. There I encountered the poorest society I had ever experienced. It was the perfect environment to test my desires theory. I was a modern soldier from the world's most advanced military and society, standing in a 17th Century-like environment. Immersed in that environment, struggling to understand it, I found that even an Afghan citizen living day to day without water, electricity and all the modern amenities and comfort I knew, had desires very similar to mine. Afghan farmers wanted to raise and grow their families in a safe environment with autonomy, free from a predatory government. The Afghan Army officers I partnered with wanted these same things. They thrived off recognition and respected discipline and authority. So did American soldiers and their families.

My study resulted in a short desires collection or "List of Six" I could use like I would a vehicle dashboard to examine my own organization and people. This dashboard became my mental model. I'm a fan of short lists, ones I can memorize and put into practice. You'll see much of Maslow's theory reflected in the words below. You could argue that I left out "Belongingness." That is fair criticism and a word perhaps you could add to your own list. I didn't have to emphasize it much given the camaraderie existing in every infantry unit I served. I considered myself lucky in that respect but didn't rest on my laurels. I chose this List of Six because it was these desires I most appreciated as a subordinate and what I found to be most effective toward building fulfilled, high-performing organizations and people. Testing this theory in the business world, I found I was not alone. Executives and professional publications like *Inc.* and *Forbes* included these desires in "Top-10" style articles. I found these desires presented as well by professional leadership organizations like Fierce, OI Global Partners and Benefits Pro to name a few. It wasn't enough to just establish a fancy list of words and move on to other busy work. I couldn't just hand this list out like pens and t-shirts to everyone who joined the team and expect results. This list required both implementation and examination to ensure it was right. Ahead, I'll define each one, share stories and offer a way for you to implement them in your organization.

· ·

List of Six

- Fulfillment
- Autonomy
- Praise & Recognition
- Safety
- Discipline
- Growth

· ·

Fulfillment. Even the best organizations will have unfulfilled
employees. As good as I know mine became, we still have several
people lacking fulfillment. When people reach something they
desire or something promised or expected, they are fulfilled. I desire
to make a difference in others, so if I were to witness the growth
of another person because of something that I did, that would
bring me great fulfillment. I placed fulfillment at the top of my list
because I feel it is central to the health of the individual and the
organization. If you can achieve fulfillment, you are really making
a difference. The goal, of course, is to have people on your team who
wake each morning excited about their day and fulfilled when they
return home. Unfortunately, the story from today's place of work is
not a pretty one. Aaron Hurst, author, and CEO of Imperative INC.,
released research in January of 2016 that claimed only 28 percent
of the 150 million-member U.S. workforce defines the role of work
in their lives primarily as a source of personal fulfillment. Another
study conducted by the Conference Board, an independent business
research firm, indicated over 50 percent of employees are dissatisfied
or unfulfilled with their job. Causes according to a *Forbes Magazine*
article "Eight Common Causes of Workplace Demotivation" can be
attributed to a lack of discipline or recourse for poor performance
(holding people accountable), lack of confidence in company leadership and ability for employees to progress. This data is alarming,
and it underscores a need for leaders and organizations to invest
in their people. Factors outside your control like bad market conditions, government regulation or even a bad relationship can stand in
the way of fulfillment. It can also be brought on by a bad supervisor,
work conditions and lack of an organizational vision and culture.
Additionally, a bad interview and hiring process may produce an
employee who is not aligned with the organization's values and
culture or who can't live out their true passion.

Though I adored my Army career, there were periods where I was unfulfilled. Most of these periods were due to a boss who failed to establish a positive work environment or invest in me. In one assignment, I felt completely unchallenged; in another, I felt like I could do nothing right, in another, my vision of combat readiness was different from my boss's. In each of those assignments, I was not the best that I could be, and it forced me to work hard to overcome this. I was less focused as a soldier. There were moments when I considered resigning and moving on to another career. What's more, I was not the best husband and father. In the Army, however, one thing was certain; the boss would soon be replaced, or you would move to a different unit. I was lucky in that respect. Had it been different, it could have taken a greater toll on me, my subordinates and my family. Along with my experience, I witnessed several family members and friends who came home from work each day disheveled and unfulfilled with their job for many of the reasons outlined above. Fear not, I believe something can be done about this, and I'll take it on from an organizational and individual level. As a leader, you will need to address both as you navigate changing environments, rotating people and social issues.

Organizational Fulfillment. Environmental conditions like the economy or a change of mission can impact fulfillment at an organizational level affecting everyone on the team. These conditions are typically out of reach for a leader to alter. Internally, aside from a bad boss or work conditions, a lack of vision or direction for the organization can create unfulfilled people. Harley Davidson's vision statement is "To fulfill dreams through the experiences of motorcycling." Employees of Harley Davidson (under great leadership) should come home each day fulfilled knowing they contributed to that vision, even if in a small way.

There were periods in my career where my organization lacked fulfillment. Our training year was divided up between focused training,
professional development and support periods. During support
periods, my unit would be tasked to conduct support missions across
the installation like guarding gates, clean up details and providing
support to units in training. Fulfillment hit rock bottom during these
periods. To overcome, I had to be ever-present amongst the soldiers
and communicate to them directly and constantly. I didn't try to
put a nice face on what every soldier disliked. I would even go as
far as expressing my own displeasure. I would tell my soldiers and
leaders that I was in the support period with them and wouldn't let
it get me down. I'd also highlight that this period would be temporary. I needed to remind the team of the great reputation we had
and how important it was for us to maintain that by showcasing our
commitment to mission accomplishment (regardless of the mission)
so that we could get back the things which brought us fulfillment like
combat-focused training.

Ways to remedy a lack of organizational fulfillment. It starts with
understanding what is causing lack of fulfillment. Once you know
that, only then can you make organizational adjustments. Next, you
should establish a positive climate in your organization. This alone
can work wonders toward achieving fulfillment among your people.
Lastly, and as a foundational approach, you must have an organizational vision, values and culture every member can subscribe to. Do
some research to determine what has changed in the environment
and poll your people to determine the effect it has had on them. If
it's environmental causes outside the reach of leaders, communication as I did with my brigade is the answer. In temporary periods,
your messaging should be about overcoming the current situation
showcasing professionalism and perseverance to weather the storm.

Where these external changes become permanent, it may call for leaders to tailor their organizations to cater to this new environment.

In Afghanistan in 2009, we were required to do more talking with local Afghans to determine causes of social unrest than we were to hunt and kill insurgents. This different mission required us to change our procedures and organizational structure to achieve effects. We needed to retrain our own forces to conduct non-lethal operations such as meeting with Afghan village, government and military leaders to determine sources of instability. We did more population assessments and embedded people like former US policemen, foreign service specialists from USAID and the Department of State as well as anthropologists into our combat patrols. To achieve fulfillment, leaders had to communicate with their soldiers about how this new approach would serve to defeat the insurgency better than a narrow concentration on killing would.

Establishing an organizational shared vision, values and culture will go a long way to achieving fulfillment. Of course, your people have to subscribe to this so you will need to either hire people who share this vision or poll your people to see who is on board and who is not. Help those who do not subscribe to depart the organization on good terms. Along with this vision, create a positive work climate and deliver on the desires I describe in my List of Six. Even if the dedicated employees of Harley Davidson believe in their vision, if the boss sets a bad tone and fosters a bad climate, the employees may become unfulfilled. In the official Army Leadership Regulation, we called organizational climates command climates, meaning, these climates were owned and managed by commanders. They measured the state of morale and level of fulfillment of unit members. Though a bit lengthy (avoid lengthy surveys), they did give decent indicators of where there was satisfaction and dissatisfaction. They told us if there was trust between soldiers and leaders and if there were issues like discrimination and harassment. I wouldn't recommend lengthy, painful surveys, but you can create specific surveys for your organization that determine the level of fulfillment and its causes. I'll cover surveys in greater detail to assist you in your fulfillment quest in Chapter 9. These surveys and sensing sessions, if done right, will do more than provide you feedback. They will tell your people you care and want to listen and invest in them. This will go a long way toward increasing fulfillment.

Individual Fulfillment. I consider individual fulfillment a harder yet more critical objective of leaders. Leaders can see organizational fulfillment through a variety of indicators and changing environments. Individual fulfillment is harder to determine, so it requires leader investment. As I stated earlier, people will desire different things so your fulfillment approach will be individualistic instead of one-size-fits-all. It starts with knowing individuals (see Chapter 7.) Use the List of Six as a template to lay over an individual to determine if he or she desires more or less autonomy or growth for example. Consider these two examples and the impact they have on people.

Dana, a father of three and a 10-year employee, was a high performer working on innovative data storage concepts for your company. He loved his duties and the mission of the company. You reward him by appointing him executive director of development placing him in charge of 12 people. What if Dana is actually very fulfilled in the position he currently holds? What if he is not interested in a raise or more responsibility? What if Dana is an introvert who thrives working alone on important data concepts but struggles when required to form and motivate a team?

Steve is a sergeant in an infantry platoon. The Army decides based on his rank and time in service that he should be a recruiter and reassigns him to recruiting duty. What if Steve, who happens to be a fantastic infantry leader, isn't a gifted orator who can easily speak to large, diverse groups of people? What if Steve does not possess natural salesman skills required to convince men and women to join the Army? What if Steve, who will now be forced to travel more often, is a father of two young children? These two scenarios might just result in unhappy, unfulfilled people who do not serve their organizations well. Furthermore, and most importantly, Dana and Steve might bring their lack of fulfillment home each day to their families.

How to remedy lack of individual fulfillment. Simple, talk to your people. This is not rocket science, but you will need to think about this deliberately before you waltz around the work area asking ill-informed questions. Simple questions like "Are you happy with your job?" might result in a lie as some employees might want to avoid the truth or not jeopardize their employment. Just like organizational fulfillment, understand the problem first. At the end of this chapter, I have provided the link to my website where I share a good, short questionnaire from Jim Hughes that measures individual professional and personal fulfillment. You will have to converse with people one-on-one to determine their personal level and you can use the results of this survey to guide your discussion. Individual counseling, short surveys and circulating to talk to people are the ways I discovered the level of fulfillment with my people. I will expand on them in Chapters 7, 8 and 9.

If it was the organization causal to their discontent, I would examine what we were doing or not doing like a bad policy or practice to contribute to their lack of fulfillment. If it was something the organization could not fix, for instance, soldier and family stability (not moving), it might require a position or career change for the individual. I could not prevent soldiers and their families from moving throughout their career. It's what made the Army work. I could, however, reverse an internal policy which caused more work for no apparent reason. There were no absolutes. Each situation required analysis, and I didn't always get it right on the first try. For instance, I had a subordinate who was very displeased with his supervisor. He claimed that a move under a new supervisor would remedy this. After a lengthy discussion with him and some others, I moved him as he desired. Things did not improve. It was him. His personality prevented him from being a good subordinate. He was brilliant and could solve complex problems, but this led him to stray from the task at hand. He needed too much supervision to keep him focused. I had to guide him toward another career.

Autonomy. Autonomy means freedom from control or oversight. A good synonym is independence. Fredrick Herzberg, Bernard Mausner and Barbra Snyderman in their book *The Motivation to Work* highlight that the more autonomy employees have at work, the more fulfilled they are in their jobs, and the less likely they are to transfer or leave their positions. I was a subordinate as much as I was a leader and I thrived under bosses who gave me the latitude and space to conduct my tasks. I have found that people desire the same. Those who desired to be told exactly what to do never worked well in any organization I led. If I had to spell each step out, they were either poorly trained or lacked the ability to operate off minimal guidance. In these cases, I was probably better suited to do the task myself. From my boss, I wanted sound instructions and intent, resources, space to complete my task and the latitude to accomplish it my way as long as I met his or her intent. I didn't always get it right. When I failed, what I appreciated most was when they would pull me aside, correct me then give me my space again. I would do anything for leaders like that. I have always tried to do this with my subordinates. As a young leader, I was guilty of telling subordinates exactly what to do. I was accused of micromanaging, and the criticism was fair. I got better at it as I matured.

There are individual prerequisites for allowing autonomy. It is centered on trust. You obviously would not give total autonomy to a new employee like you would a seasoned one. You have to establish trust and determine ability and capability. This requires hiring people who thrive on autonomy and providing education and training and supervision early in their tenure. For young or new subordinates, depending on the mission, my range of autonomy would vary. For instance, if it were a mission of critical importance I would probably supervise or take more briefings from the individual to ensure my intent was understood. For those tasks of lesser criticality, I would allow more space. I wanted to get to a place where I could allow almost total autonomy so I might assign easier tasks to allow for greater autonomy earlier in the relationship.

Practicing autonomy with your subordinates does not mean turning your back completely. I have seen that approach and the catastrophic results of it. Surely, there is a sweet spot, and this depends largely on the individual and the task. It is our duty as leaders to check to ensure tasks are being completed to standard. Some leaders want to avoid confrontation, so they steer clear of the task as it is being conducted. Some do this out of laziness. The worst scenario is to arrive upon task completion only to learn it was done wrong and must be redone. Aside from the waste of time and effort, you will all but ensure employee resentment.

How to foster autonomy. My autonomy approach: Give them my vision and intent and get out of their way. The key to fostering autonomy in your organization is sound intent. Note that I did not say instructions or use 'how to.' Though it was tempting to tell people exactly how I wanted things to be accomplished, I knew I had to avoid this. Even as a brigade commander, I would catch myself telling a subordinate how to "suck the egg" as we would often say. I would stop myself, place my hand on their shoulder, re-issue my intent and tell them I trusted them. General George S. Patton famously said, "Don't tell people how to do things, tell them what to do and let them surprise you with their results." As a commander, I placed my emphasis, not on the specifics of how I wanted something done but rather how I would issue my intent. This was everything, especially as a senior leader because I wouldn't always have the opportunity to issue it in person. For intent, I used the framework the Army taught me outlined in the Army Mission Command publication: *Purpose* (the why behind the task), *Key Tasks* (important tasks which needed to be completed to meet my desired end state) and *End State* (how it should look, feel, sound, etc., when complete). The most important part of intent, in my assessment, is *purpose*. We owe our people the *purpose* or *why* behind what we tell them to do so they can put their creative minds behind the task. If the mission is reforming the personal data sheet for the company, tell Sarah the *purpose* behind that task is so you can be a better servant leader to your people. If she is a smart, dependable, independent person, she can do a lot with this statement. She will keep this goal in mind throughout her work developing a new data sheet.

For *key tasks*, you cannot possibly include all the tasks required for a mission, so include those you know to be essential, meaning without their completion, the mission would fail. For Sarah's mission, some *key tasks* could be to ensure the data sheet is password protected, easy to complete, and includes pertinent family information. These tasks would lie at the core of the mission keeping the form private and short preventing disgruntled employees. Moreover, it would include family data allowing the leader to know about and ask about people important to the employee. In another example, a mission to seize a bridge to allow the passage of critical engineer units (*purpose*) for missions deeper in the combat zone. Artillery support and the link up of bridge assessment teams might be two key tasks to achieve an end state of bridge seizure and serviceability.

End state, I always found, was the most challenging for me to verbalize appropriately yet it was important to promote autonomy. Here, you have to describe your vision of successful mission accomplishment. For Sarah's personal data sheet mission, end state would be "a brief, password-protected, useful document that is both easy to fill out and that helps leaders be servant leaders to their people." For the bridge seizure, *end state* would have the bridge and its surrounding area seized, secured and the bridge assessed to determine if heavy engineer equipment could travel over it. Your intent statement should be able to stand alone. Whether in written or verbal form, it was always helpful for me to have a conversation, if possible, with the individual tasked to ensure understanding and take general feedback and ideas. Give Sarah her task, get out of her way and let her meet your end state as she desires. It is okay to inspect along the way or require an in-progress review but try not to interfere. Get intent right, and you can promote autonomy in your organization. Your people will appreciate it.

Praise and recognition. Praise and recognition need to be offered regularly to have an enduring impact on employee engagement. For proof, look no further than Gallup's research which indicates that employees who report that they are not adequately recognized at work are three times more likely to say they will leave in the following year. *The Training Journal*, a London-based professional development publication, highlights that being praised triggers the release of dopamine, a neurotransmitter that helps control the reward and pleasure centers of the brain. As well as making us feel good, dopamine can also contribute to innovative thinking and creative problem-solving at work.

Praise and recognition are things we so often miss but which create healthy people and work environments. Coupled with the benefits listed above, numerous studies have shown the direct correlation of improved productivity and combat readiness to praise and recognition. Often in businesses, leaders believe that pay, benefits and entitlements are enough to motivate our employees and soldiers. Wouldn't a raise or some time off encourage an increase in productivity or readiness? While money and benefits are important, if you believe this approach is the only answer, you're missing it.

Each of us has someone we want to please. Even deep into our adult years many of us still desire the approval of and recognition from our parents. Most want to please their boss and their peers in an organization. Praise and recognition tell us we have succeeded. They tell us we are valued. I always appreciated being thanked or recognized for my accomplishments. I was even more grateful when my family was recognized. They were the center of my world, and I succeeded at nothing without their love and support. Praise and recognition caused me to rededicate myself to my boss and to the organization. My loyalty and motivation improved and I would work even harder. My family would feel more connected to the organization, and my spouse would communicate more with my leaders and feel more inclined to participate and volunteer in unit activities. I've witnessed the same with soldiers. Talk about return on investment; Just a simple pat on the back, a thanks or certificate of achievement and recognition of family members resulted in an increase in soldier performance and family inclusion in unit activities. I witnessed several cases where this would occur. My leaders, noticing a positive change would often ask what I said or did to the soldier. My usual response was "I just thanked him and his family and told them how important they were to the unit." It went a very long way toward keeping good soldiers and their loving families on the Army team. I conducted praise and recognition often, both formally and informally at the organizational and individual level and even though I knew its importance, I was still amazed at the positive reaction.

The Army has some great formal traditions to foster praise and recognition which you can emulate and a generous inventory of ribbons, medals and official certificates to make events special and provide lasting impact. Every month, most units host an event called a Hail and Farewell. Here, unit leaders and their families gather in a social setting to welcome or farewell unit members. For senior officers and NCOs, units may host a formal ceremony with soldiers on parade. These events mark the important transition of key leaders in an organization and provide an opportunity to recognize the accomplishments of the departing leader and family and significance of the arrival of the new member and his or her family. Traditionally (though not always the case), soldiers receive an award for their service in a unit upon their departure. For specific achievements, leaders could award soldiers with medals and certificates. Normally units would present awards in a large formal assembly where the recipients get to stand in front of their comrades. Leaders of smaller organizations such as company-sized units and above usually have unit coins (medal medallions emblazoned with unit symbols) they hand out for excellent performance. The Army even has medals for spouses to recognize their support, sacrifice and volunteer efforts. Most every Army installation hosts an Army Family of the Quarter or Year at formal ceremonies to recognize the importance of Army families. When soldiers reenlist, an officer will conduct the reading of the oath with comrades and family members present to recognize and celebrate service to the nation. I'm proud to highlight all that the Army does to award its deserving soldiers and family members. Aside from a parade of rifle-toting soldiers, businesses can replicate all that I have described. Many do and they are an important part of investing in people.

How to conduct praise and recognition. I leveraged all our formal traditions to praise and recognize my people and their families but also sought unplanned opportunities as often as I could. Make your desire to praise and recognize your people known with your subordinate leaders. I made this very clear with my leaders and offered my personal time. They took me up on this offer. One event had significant impact. While visiting soldiers in training, I conducted an official reenlistment ceremony in the back of a helicopter, symbolic of our profession, in full combat gear. Pictures from the event went viral and motivation went through the roof. A few moments of my time resulted in a huge investment. I kept unit coins nearby as well as a stack of thank you notes and as I traveled the unit and connected with people I would take opportunities to recognize them. I could either award a coin on the spot or follow with a personal note. I always found personal notes to be significant. These notes displayed my gratitude and the time I took to write and send the note. They said a lot. I still have some personal thank you notes given to me from people I respected.

Give this a shot. At the organizational level, establish a formal recognition ceremony monthly or quarterly and include family members. Create your own inventory of medals, ribbons and certificates which you can award for excellence. Establish policies and plan reoccurring events which prevent people from being forgotten for all the hard work they do. Outline how you will welcome your people into the organization and how you will send them off with dignity recognizing their contributions. Get creative. Take a small group of individuals to a museum or a statue near you which reflects the dedication and performance of the person you are recognizing. Have the group assemble near the first of a new product or web design or invite in a customer who was particularly happy with their experience and recognize your people. Look for opportunities to include and recognize family members. Send a note home for a spouse or significant other remarking on how much you value their loved one and their support of him or her. For individual praise and recognition, create a reporting requirement for subordinate leaders to highlight their superstars for you. Talk often about how much you want to recognize your people. Your leaders will listen and help you do this. Book some time daily or weekly to walk your area and thank your people. Lastly, get to know your people. You will know better those who thrive off praise and recognition and you will be better prepared to do this.

Safety. I use safety in my List of Six not in the sense of creating physically safe environments at work like locked doors, lighting in hallways and fire drills. That is certainly imperative but I use it as a sense of being or a psychological state where people are comfortable from threats like being fired after making an innocent mistake or scolded for speaking their mind or preyed upon by an outside organization or a higher-level supervisor. In an article called "The Magic of Feeling Safe," Tony Schwartz states; "When we feel emotionally unsafe at work, our fight or flight instincts kick in and our ability to think logically and reflectively diminish. Some may shut down, unwilling to contribute to anything productive, cautiously navigating their way through their work days."

I worked once for a boss once who was very hard to please. The staff, who supported him and the organization, were afraid to present anything to him for fear that he would berate them for poor staff work. I became protective of the staff and where I could I would present products and analysis to him myself. This leadership approach resulted in members of the organization who were afraid to speak up and challenge anything they believed needed to be challenged. Staff contribution was minimal as members believed no amount of extra dedication and effort would please the boss. When being criticized many of the staff members would shut down and take the abuse. Both the organization and its people suffered as a result of not feeling safe in the workplace.

The tale of two Maggies. Our first Maggie went into work on Tuesday and hit traffic on the way. She suffered a minor panic attack and could not finish her coffee and breakfast she'd brought along for her commute. She had been late a few months ago and was berated by her boss in front of her peers in a meeting. Thankfully, she got through the traffic and arrived on time. Peering across the office, she sees that her boss is in his office surrounded by a few people with a phone to his ear engaged deep in conversation. Thankful he is tied up and cannot call out to her as he usually does, she gets past his view and arrives in her office to the relative safety behind her desk and computer screen. Her momentary comfort quickly fades as she starts up her computer and opens her email. Her discomfort returns as her email loads figuring she will have the daily batch of curt messages from her boss. Later that morning in their daily meeting, she listens as her boss rambles on about current tasks, new ones and what is expected of everyone. She listens but cannot help but think about the error he made in one of his emails this morning which could derail the upcoming marketing campaign. She had some great cost-saving product improvement ideas for today's meeting and wanted to share them with the team but she is consumed by how she will correct her boss's morning error in this open forum. Knowing she has to correct the error to prevent failure before everyone departs the meeting she speaks up when it is her turn. Her boss is angered over the correction and fires back defending his actions attempting to turn the blame on to Maggie. Maggie counters with a meager defense but knows she can only push so hard. She fears she will lose her job if she challenges her boss. She fears that he will poison her reputation if she decides to resign and find work elsewhere. The meeting ends and Maggie quickly makes her way back to the relative safety of her office. She checks her watch hoping that it is close to lunch so she can escape the office for a short while to eat in her car where she knows her boss won't find her.

Our second Maggie hits traffic on the way into work on Tuesday but handles it calmly. Aside from her frustration over the traffic, Maggie knows her boss does not monitor her comings and goings. He knows she is a dedicated employee and works extra hard for the betterment of the company. Maggie turns up the radio and finishes her coffee and breakfast. Arriving at work on time, she walks through the office to see her boss surrounded by people with a phone to his ear. He notices her arrival and smiles and waves at her. Maggie arrives at her office, sits back and opens up her email. There is a string of messages from her boss but she already knows he is not one to get emotional on email and does not expect immediate responses unless he asks. From her previous interactions with him, he would rather hear from her personally if there is an issue. His door is always open. Later that morning in the meeting, her boss opens by telling an amusing story about his clumsiness in spilling a cup of coffee during his conference call with the CEO then provides updates on a variety of topics. Once he is complete, he sits back and asks for feedback from all the meeting members. People speak up sharing their thoughts on his updates. Maggie, noticing the error from the morning's email string corrects her boss. He is immediately grateful and asks what should be done. Maggie offers a quick and easy solution and her boss makes a few notes as she speaks. Maggie offers to fix the error herself as she has seen it happen before. Her boss thanks her and takes a moment to remind everyone he thrives off group think and expects that people will challenge and correct him as Maggie has done for the benefit of the organization. Maggie then shares her cost-saving product improvement ideas with the team which starts an open debate amongst the attendees. Her boss asks a few questions during the debate and allows all members to be heard. The meeting ends and people slowly depart engaging in casual conversation. When lunch comes, Maggie heads over to the employee lounge hoping that her coworkers and boss are around so she can catch up with them to see what they have planned for the upcoming holiday. On her way home that evening, Maggie's boss thanks her for the morning correction and asks what she has planned for the upcoming holiday. Hearing her plans, he suggests they move the morning update earlier so that she has some extra time to pack for her flight later that day.

Now guess which environment is safe and which is not? Our first Maggie, while not displaying any fear or angst, is tormented by her daily work experience. Her cost-saving-idea is never heard. She is more interested in protecting herself and escaping the meeting environment instead of sharing something she knows will benefit the team. She avoids socializing at work for fear her boss will interrupt and berate her or add to her task list. Instead she hides in her vehicle. She is likely not sleeping well and is not a good wife to her husband because of all her work stress. Our second Maggie heads to work eager to connect with her boss and co-workers. She knows her sage advice will get the attention it deserves. She feels completely safe coming and going from work and approaching her boss with practically any topic. She feels safe correcting her boss when needed as she knows he has the organization and his people foremost in his mind and not himself. She is happy and healthy and full of energy each day.

How to promote safety in your organization. Leaders set tone. This is perhaps the most important part of fostering safety in your work place. I did many things in my organization to ensure my people felt safe. My efforts typically fell into these five categories:

1. Displaying a calm demeanor.

2. Openness to ideas, encouraging subordinates to share ideas and disagree with me.

3. Transparent leadership, sharing my weaknesses.

4. Giving credit where it is due

5. Protecting your team or individuals from outside influencers.

I started by setting tone. Leaders set tone by all that they say and do. I always had a calm demeanor. There were times when I became upset and times when I had to be stern with a subordinate in a public forum but I would always handle myself maturely. I was not a hothead. Constantly, I reminded people I wanted to hear their opinions and analysis. I wanted divergent thinking. With my rank and position many were reluctant to speak up. I had to demonstrate that I was willing to listen and wanted to hear from them. My humility was helpful in creating a safe environment. I was not afraid to expose my weaknesses and even my clumsiness. I made an effort to include the ideas of my subordinates into plans and I would give them credit. I had a brilliant planner and intelligence officer who created some superb analysis. I used it often and credited them for generating it. When things went wrong or we as an organization failed, instead of rushing to pin blame, I would turn the failure into an opportunity to learn. I'd quickly assemble those involved and work through what caused the failure so we could prevent repeat. I stuck up for my team when outside influences began to impact them in a negative way. If it were a person in a higher headquarters or my boss, I would offer top cover to my people taking blame for their mistakes or defending them if necessary. I championed their personal and professional goals and communicated with HRC to ensure they saw them as I did. Replicate this in your organization. Be the leader who creates and owns a safe work environment. Stick up for your people and be their champion.

Discipline. Discipline is doing the right thing when nobody is looking. More formal definitions describe discipline as training people to obey a set of rules punishing those who do not. Discipline is an essential ingredient to any organization whether flat and decentralized or structured and hierarchical like the Army. Without it, the organization suffers lack of productivity, efficiency or even injury or loss of life. Whether soldier or civilian, people desire discipline in the work place. Think about a workplace without it. Consider the behavior of the undisciplined soldiers in Iraq in Abu Ghraib Prison. They belonged to an organization that lacked discipline. Think about a work environment where poor performance or violations of rules go uncorrected and unpunished.

In the Army, my teammates and I wanted to be held to a standard which permeated the organization, and we wanted it enforced. When we learned of misconduct, especially in leaders, we sought fair punishment. As leaders, we were always challenged to correct violations on the spot instead of walking by them. This does not mean it's time to rush out and purchase a drill sergeant hat and whistle. It also doesn't mean you should establish martial law or an overly strict work environment. I never wanted to be around a boss who instilled discipline through fear. That can lead to toxicity. I always strove to create an environment where people were comfortable, especially in the military, but when it came to indiscipline, I dealt with it rapidly and fairly. People expect this of leaders. In the Army, strict grooming and uniform guidelines and codes of conduct are examples of the standards which promote an environment of discipline essential in a unit which may see combat. A break from these standards leads directly to a degradation in discipline that in combat can have fatal consequences. The same holds true in business. When standards and discipline slip, so does everything else.

As a commander to promote discipline, I rendered punishment under the Uniform Code of Military Justice (UCMJ). This code was created to instill justice and good order and discipline. When a soldier knowingly violated an article of the UCMJ we could reduce him or her in rank, garnish pay and place restrictions on their freedoms. This code was a helpful tool to instill good order and discipline, but I used it very deliberately. I didn't rush to punishment. We also didn't hold court every time there was a violation. In many cases, initial violations could be addressed with an on-the-spot correction and a formal counseling statement to document the infraction. Whenever there was a shade of doubt, before punishment, I would investigate formally. I always sought the advice of my lawyer. I took punishments very seriously and wanted to ensure they followed the law and were fair. Punishments, though issued to a soldier, served a greater purpose. When they were issued, the organization would learn of them and know that we took misconduct very seriously.

A leader's role in instilling good order and discipline is stewardship of the organization its values and or the profession over self. I took my role as a steward of the Army profession very seriously. Like almost everything I did, it was all about the organization and the mission before it was about an individual. Almost always, I would hold Army values above a soldier who committed an offense. There might be exceptions such as combat trauma (organization caused) which may have been causal to the misconduct. I found these to be the exception. I once rendered punishment on a soldier I held in very high regard. It was a difficult decision, and I was completely blindsided by the misconduct, but I was given a choice; show leniency on an individual and disregard all the Army stood for or render punishment fitting the offense to show my loyalty to the Army and its standards.

I chose the latter because I was a steward of the Army profession. I made stewardship a key teaching point in my development of younger officers and promoted it in my brigade.

I took no pleasure in rendering punishment. I wanted to address causes. What I desired the most was to learn why the misconduct happened in the first place. I wanted to get to the cause of the problem (reason: soldier violated code) instead of the symptom (violation). Was it a lack of policy, leader presence, or organizational climate-related? Many violations were worthy of punishment, but if we could address the cause(s), then we might prevent re-occurrence. Punishing a soldier was easy. Trying to address his or her problems was a challenge, and I wanted to take that on. It would require an investment in the person. Because discipline was so important, I held a leader forum in my brigade where we could discuss misconduct and attempt to discover causes. We called it Soldiers of Concern, and I will discuss it more in Chapter 4.

How to instill discipline in your organization. You do not have to have the UCMJ, high-and-tight haircuts and starched uniforms in your business to instill discipline. You should, however, strive to live by standards like a code of conduct and values. You should hold violators accountable. It starts with your organizational vision and values. Your people must have guidance for their conduct in the organization, and if you start with a vision complete with values, it becomes the code for your organization, one which you and your subordinate leaders should enforce. Make your standards known across your organization and become the steward of these standards. Espouse them in all that you do. For instance, if customer service is one of the organization's top priorities then employees should be disciplined in their efforts to ensure it is upheld. Or if integrity and discretion are top employee values of a business where customers share sensitive personal information, then leaders must instill this discipline in the organization's members and punish those who violate these values. When you have violators, take a deliberate approach to addressing violations. Seek professional counsel before investigating violations and rendering punishment. Either develop punishment options or know what options already exist. Don't rush toward life in prison! A written reprimand may send a strong enough message instead of demoting or firing someone. Whichever form of punishment you chose always ask yourself if the punishment helps foster good discipline in your organization. Attempt to correct personal behavior addressing formally with an individual what caused the misconduct and/or adjust organizational policies and practices instead of just handing out punishments. Work with your team to determine root causes of indiscipline and misconduct.

The chain of command. In the Army, we have rank structure and the chain of command to help separate superiors from subordinates. Rank is one of the first things you learn in your accession into the service. Separation of rank was a very important element of establishing discipline. Your voice could be heard if you were of lower rank, but when it came time for discipline, the senior officer or NCO held the position and rank authority. As a young organizational leader commanding a 24-man unit, I allowed myself to get too close with my subordinates. The walls of rank came down, and I had difficulty when it came to instilling discipline. I was too friendly with my men, and I failed to maintain my rank and position separate from my soldiers. Thankfully, a very good NCO arrived to serve as my second in command and re-established the rank structure in the organization.

You do not have to don military-style rank and refer to each other as sergeant or colonel in your organization, but I offer caution in becoming too close and operating without any organizational structure. Environments, where subordinates and superiors are on a first name basis, are healthy, however, if you are the boss or supervisor then you should both act like one and be known as one. There should be titles in your organization that bring with them authority and structure. For instance, Scott may be referred to by his first name by his subordinates, but his official position, known to all is the Executive Vice President of Marketing. This does not mean you cannot intermingle or socialize with your employees. You just have to be cautious of becoming too close. It happens to be one of the burdens of leadership. I socialized with my subordinates throughout my career, and I strongly suggest you do as well but remember to keep your bearing as the boss. In the Army, we always called each other by our rank, and though we were in civilian uniform, we kept our military bearing. This is a fine line especially if you desire to get to know your people and the hardest part of your investment. Use this as your measurement; would you feel comfortable rendering punishment or firing a subordinate of yours if he or she failed to achieve results, violated organizational rules or policies or just failed to perform well? While punishment is never an easy task if your friendship with a subordinate would make it difficult for you to instill discipline or correct his or her actions or behavior, you may have a problem with authority and position in your organization so critical to fostering an environment of order and discipline.

Lastly, get to know your people. Refer to what's in Chapter 6. If you would rather invest in them instead of just punishing them, then start by getting to know them. You might just be able to prevent misconduct, or if it happens, you might be able to address a root cause. We could not fix every soldier in the Army. Some we had to separate from service. We had a saying in the Army, "You spend 90 percent of your time on 10 percent of your soldiers." If you or your subordinate leaders know the 10 percent, you can decide quicker if they can be repaired or if they need to leave for the betterment of the organization. Nothing brings unfulfillment in an organization more than a bad apple who continues to under-perform or misbehave. If you do this right, you can nurture a disciplined work environment. If you approach it haphazardly or not at all, indiscipline will fester, and bad things will come. Your attention will be paid to the 10 percent instead of the 90 percent who deserve it.

Growth. The word growth is often used synonymously with development. Cornerstone, a talent management organization, defined employee development as a process where the employee with the support of his or her employer undergoes various training programs to enhance his or her skills and acquire new knowledge and skills. I'll take this a step further and add personal development (growth). Making people better people involves both personal and professional growth. My personal life always affected my career, and I knew that I needed to grow personally and professionally. Because of this, I wanted to discuss it with those I counseled.

There is nothing worse than a person gone stale or a work environment not conducive to growth. Indra Nooyi, the CEO of PepsiCo posits that CEOs and employees should be "a student for life" as one of her top lessons featured in an article she published highlighting what she's learned from a decade as a CEO. People are constantly growing physically and mentally, and it is up to us as leaders to champion this growth and prevent stagnation. Stale employees, who are prevented from achieving personal and professional growth, can be very detrimental to an organization. Think about it, would you rather have an employee who is actively growing, looking to the future and trying to improve or someone who shows up just to complete his or her tasks? While there are some people who are content with stagnation, your organization is mostly full of those who desire personal and professional growth. I was fortunate as an Army officer because the Army continued to invest in me throughout my career constantly sending me to school and allowing me to advance in rank and responsibility. The Army also placed me in numerous environments where I had to learn the local customs and cultures. I recall only short periods in my career where I began to grow stale.

Regardless of where I was in my career, I always had a goal and/or passion in mind. Professionally, as a younger officer, I wanted to earn a master's degree. Personally, I always had a goal of riding my motorcycle on an adventure like a trip to the Arctic Circle. I want to write a book and visit more countries. I want to learn a second language. I desire to mature and grow as a father to my two sons who will soon finish college. I want to help small businesses invest in their people. Each of these desires equates to growth for me personally and professionally. I am happy to say that I have accomplished some of them and thankfully I had a few leaders along the way who helped. Throughout my career, though, I did some growing on my own and grew through experiencing challenging situations. I would have loved a leader who was fully engaged with me and my desires. I would have loved a leader who challenged me to realize my goals and who offered methods and resources to achieve them. I had a few but not enough.

How to grow your people. When I took command of my brigade, my plan was not to rely solely on the Army to grow my people. I wanted to grow them myself. It was both a passion and my duty as their leader. I approached this by considering the answer to a few simple questions.

- What personal and professional growth does this person in front of me require?
- Do they themselves know?
- What are they doing to grow themselves?
- What can I do to assist?

I considered obtaining the answer to these questions my personal challenge. I wanted constant knowledge so I could grow my people. Through my time working with and counseling them I would be able to answer these questions and, better yet, do what I could to help. In all my formal counseling and in discussions with leaders and soldiers, I would always ask what was next for them. This would lead to a great conversation where I could get to know them better and help them realize their need for growth. I could then ask what they were doing to help themselves achieve their goal(s). If getting married and starting a family or obtaining a master's degree was one, I could offer advice having done that myself. If I found they had no good answer to these questions, I could challenge them and help them discover gaps in their growth and create a path toward achievement.

Be without boundaries when thinking about how to help grow an employee. Take personal goals just as seriously as you would professional ones. If they wanted to obtain an advanced degree not specifically related to the organization's mission, help them anyway. Give them some time off to attend classes and keep them on goal or help fund the degree. If they've always wanted to skydive, help them achieve that. You have to think outside the walls of your organization. Place your loyalty to the growth of your people over the needs of your organization. If one of your subordinates has met or exceeded all the requirements of his or her current position and there is no way up for them in your organization, allow them to grow somewhere else. Help them find that place. For example, one time I was asked to provide names for candidates to serve as an aide to a general. I picked one of my very best officers who I had identified to serve as my executive officer. This would have hurt me badly, but it would have enhanced the officer's career far more than I could inside my own organization. I would be able to find another qualified candidate to fill the

position, so I placed the officer's growth above my brigade's needs.
I even coached some officers to leave the Army or pursue another
career path. It was rare that I would do this, especially for a talented
individual but their growth was my goal and the right investment
to make. The alternative could have negative effects. For the very
best of our employees, we hope that path keeps them on our team.
Regardless, the greater good is a healthier, more content person. I'll
take that over anything.

Closing. As you might go to great lengths developing a program or
process which speeds production, cuts costs or helps your organization maintain its weapons better, you should apply this same weight
to investing in your people. Few, if any programs, in government
and business can succeed without fulfilled people in disciplined,
safe, growth environments where people are praised, recognized
and enjoy autonomy. If you want your subordinates to think and act
as you would conducting their daily duties or serving in harm's way
far from your supervision, first understand their importance then
make attainment of their desires your mission. They are not weapons
or websites. Keep their importance and desires foremost in your
mind each day.

Visit *www.RobCampbellLeadership.com/Book* for additional material
on the desires of people, a tool to measure personal and professional
fulfillment and how to issue intent-based instructions.

Chapter 4
ESTABLISHING THE FOUNDATION FOR INVESTING IN PEOPLE

Now, I know you are at the drive-thru window ready to order a number three meal "Investing in People" supersized. You are ready to consume it, press the easy button and get started. However, we need to build the foundation to the house first. This is where it gets uncomfortable. Yes, you are going to have to back out of the drive-thru, anger a bunch of hungry people and park your car over in the corner of the fast food parking lot to work through this. You can elect to begin right now building an "Investing in People" house by connecting with your people through various methods and programs, but the house will sag or even collapse if you fail to get the foundation right. Your impatience may lead you to create a counseling program or host a self-awareness seminar (or hire an agency to do it) and engage in some introspection. These efforts would produce positive results, but they will be short-lived if you do not pour a solid foundation upon which they can rest and draw strength. Everything I did in my brigade and every success we enjoyed could be traced back to my first day in command when my subordinate leaders and I built a foundation, specifically our shared brigade vision. I spent a considerable amount of time preparing for this first session with my leaders because I knew the outcome was vital to the future of the brigade. We would be embarking on a people-centric endeavor for an organization nearly 5,000 in size. There are three ingredients to this foundation we are about to pour. It starts with you, rests on your organization's vision and requires the establishment of priorities. Here is the list from one of the many Army green notebooks I carried in my career.

- You
- Organizational Vision (Values and Culture)
- Priorities

YOU

First test: you have to be the right person. Really. Let's leave the drive-thru jokes in the last paragraph. You may not be the right person. If you are not, then step aside or surround yourself with people who can carry out an investing in people campaign for you. Either way, it is going to be difficult if you are not the right person. As a brigade commander, responsible for some 5,000 soldiers and their families, I walked through the door of my headquarters each day a different person than the one who walked into his house at the end of the day. At home, I was Rob or Dad the guy (with much less authority!) who would let his guard down completely, joke and have fun in the house with my wife and sons. At work, I was Colonel Campbell or "Sir," a seasoned senior Army leader with enormous responsibility and authority who commanded respect. The key was this; I was comfortable being that person who entered the brigade headquarters. I didn't have to fake it or work hard to be someone

I was not. It humbled me but my authority and position and all that came with it felt real and purposeful. Those who felt alien as they walked into their building were the wrong people for the position. Some recognized this and departed the Army on another path. Others either suppressed their feelings or became someone not true to themselves. Living a lie surfaces at some point and it can be pretty ugly when it does.

To illustrate, I relieved a few company (small subordinate, stand-alone franchises of 100-120 soldiers) commanders because they were unfit to lead their organizations. They hadn't violated our code, ethics or policies; they were just the wrong person. When I counseled them and their superiors I found they did not possess the traits and characteristics required for them to succeed. Some failed to connect to their people, some communicated very poorly, some did not listen to superiors and subordinates and repeated mistakes. This didn't make them bad people, just the wrong people in the wrong place. One commander, in particular, was working too hard to be the officer he thought he should be because it was the typical path his peers had taken. It was the path the Army expected him to take as a combat arms officer. After a lengthy discussion trying to discover his true passion, a look of relief came over his face. He found peace knowing he did not have to follow a certain career path just because his peers had. He was different, not bad or less of a person, just different. He had strong introvert traits. He was raised by a father who worked as an intelligence analyst doing much of his work in small cells away from people. This officer possessed the intellect but struggled connecting to people. It all came crumbling down during a training exercise where he was thrust into a challenging scenario requiring him to be who he was not. Personally, I liked this officer and saw a lot of potential in him, just not in the combat arms field as a company commander. Perhaps the Army missed this shortfall in his accession into the combat arms field. I certainly missed it in a few officers who I placed into command. It's because I had not invested in them well enough.

Look at this list of traits and characteristics outlined below. Note that a characteristic refers to the distinguishing qualities that make up an individual and a trait is a feature of an individual that is inherited. The main difference between a characteristic and a trait is while a characteristic needs to be built by a person, a trait comes from your family upbringing. I'll offer this simple example. Strong emotions may be a trait you possess. That is something you likely gained in your upbringing. It doesn't mean you are unfit for the job. You may just have to be more conscious of how your emotions spike and what you need to do to manage it so you can lead effectively. I was a seasoned leader when I took over my brigade. I had a strong sense of humor which was a trait I learned in my upbringing. This sense of humor was not always a good fit in a very serious profession. I had to consciously wrestle with that as a commander. Considering characteristics, I had great listening characteristics that improved as I aged as a leader. For instance, I would talk less and follow where the communicator wanted to take me instead of guiding him or her myself. This leadership characteristic came through years of training, education and practice.

Once more, you have to be the right person. List time again. This one below served less as a daily checklist and more as a framework I could use to measure people myself and allow them to do the same. In some counseling sessions, I would present this list, and we would discuss it. In the cases where I had to relieve an officer, it was often this list I used to demonstrate to the officer where he or she went wrong. Does this list below describe you?

- Selfless

- Humble
- Brave
- Good listener
- Self-Aware

I'm a fan of short lists. You could add energetic, trustworthy, ethical, optimistic, fast learner, etc., but I'll leave you with this list to guide your investing in people journey. Just for clarity sake, I'll call these characteristics but whatever you call them, or if you choose to determine whether the individual was born with them or developed them over time, to me all that matters less. I chose these characteristics because they are the personal ingredients required for a leader who wishes to invest in his people. They are the leader's foundation. I certainly wanted my leaders to be ethical and trustworthy, but I assumed they were already. If I found they were not, I would confront that before serving a day under their leadership. Reflecting back on my 27-year career, these were the personal ingredients I would pick for leaders I wanted to serve with. Leaders who failed to invest in me or their people lacked some or all of these. Those who excelled possessed these in abundance. Each of them deserves discussion, and I'll dedicate that time in the pages ahead.

Selfless. Being selfless quite simply means placing the needs of others and of the organization above your own. Even in the Army where we promote selfless service in every leadership course and in our core Army Values, I've found a few leaders along my journey who talked a good game but who definitely put themselves first. They would promote their personal accomplishments before their subordinates, steer their organizations toward efforts that made them personally look good and seek the spotlight when their leader came around. They were quick to criticize their peers behind their back. We called them self-servers or smiling monkeys. The superiors of smiling monkeys look down and see a monkey, smiling, working hard and climbing upward. Subordinates look up and see an ass. These smiling monkeys would please their boss even at the cost of their own organization and its people. The Army caught a few of them and sent them away. Some operated under the radar. Their boss likely didn't see their selfishness but their subordinates sure could. You cannot hide that in an organization. People are smart and will see right through you. Do not be a smiling monkey. We all have selfish tendencies. Each of us wants to please our boss or higher headquarters and sometimes cost incurred by our own organizations, and their people are worth it. It's how we act upon our selfish tendencies which make the difference. Your best defense against your own selfishness is consciousness of it. When it rears its ugly head, beat it down or have a co-worker, friend or fellow soldier help you overcome. Often when I felt selfish tendencies come on such as reaping a benefit my soldiers would not have like time off, a heated vehicle or a beer, I would discuss it with my Command Sergeant Major (CSM), my senior enlisted soldier and closest professional confidant. We would assess our position in the organization, what we were being called upon to do, analyze fairness and decide how best to act.

Humble. I always defined humble as having a tempered or modest opinion of your own importance. Some would confuse it with a lack of confidence, but I actually believe it takes confidence and bravery to be humble. I always appreciated working for leaders who could keep their ego in check. By nature, I am a humble person. I was able to display my humility in several ways like laughing at myself among my teammates when I did something particularly clumsy. I would often mention how I was not the smartest in the room having graduated college with a 2.6 GPA. Though humble, I did have to be very conscious of my ego. I do have a big ego. Imagine if you will, standing in front of some 5,000 soldiers or leading them in a helicopter assault.

It's hard not to have an ego as an Army Colonel and commander of infantry soldiers or as a CEO with the big office and hiring and firing authority.

The human ego, which is our sense of self-esteem or self-importance, is a living breathing beast inside each of us. I confess I didn't really understand the human ego until my wife picked up Eckhart Tolle's book, *A New Earth, Awakening Your Life's Purpose.* It was deep but fantastic. Tolle defines the human ego as if it was a living being and describes how it affects our behavior. The ego, Tolle states wants to be nurtured so it can thrive in our subconscious self. When we strive to be right and want others to be wrong, when we complain or resent or try to feel superior, it is our ego at work. Tolle attempts to instill a sense of consciousness in the reader to defeat the trappings of the ego. It spoke to me as I could see my own behavior and that of others for what it really was. When I read about it, I could instantly picture leaders I had served with, acquaintances and family members and even myself.

My ego was fighting its way to the surface and wanted nothing to do with my humility. It was frequently hungry and desired to be fed. For dinner, it wanted to be always right, ignore others, highlight their weaknesses, complain and never apologize. For dessert, it desired a big helping of lack of patience and empathy. My ego escaped a few times, I confess, (and it still does) but because of a new level of consciousness, I was able to suppress it. This suppression remains a fight to this day when my ego attempts to escape. It's a powerful force which we as leaders must understand and manage. If not, we place ourselves and our organizations at risk.

Along with consciousness, I always found just thinking about the enormity of my position helpful. I was charged with the care of some 5,000 soldiers and their families and might lead the organization in combat. I could end careers with a few words on an efficiency report and change lives forever with the smallest decisions. This responsibility humbled me perhaps more than anything. It kept me grateful and dedicated toward achieving my mission and caring for my people. You do not have to lead 5,000 people to find humility, just being labeled a leader or having people in your charge, whether five or 5,000 ought to do the trick. Strive for consciousness in your leadership role. Consider the impact you make on people's lives. Be humble and not afraid to share your weaknesses. If you genuinely care for your people, they will see past your weaknesses, appreciate your humility and follow you anywhere.

Brave. Bravery is the willingness to face danger or difficulty. To invest in people right you will have to overcome some natural fear. You will have to look people in the eye and tell them how disappointed you are in their performance. You will have to battle back the ego monster. You will have to stand up to superiors when it is right to defend your teammates. You will have to open up and share your personal weaknesses and admit when you are wrong.

Most people are uncomfortable or afraid to do those things. I was no exception. I volunteered to serve in the Army knowing I would serve in places like Afghanistan surrounded by insurgents who wanted to kill me. That certainly took some bravery, but I still had to muster the courage to overcome all these requirements of investing in people. Bravery was required to look people in the eye, some older than I, and say what needed to be said. I had to overcome the fear of exposing my weaknesses and details about my personal life, and I had to possess the courage to apologize and admit fault when I had done wrong. I'm not alone. I have seen Army generals who could not overcome their fear, who become nervous and visibly uncomfortable when counseling. If you cower or hand the hard tasks off to others, you may not be fit for this journey.

Because counseling was the most frequent activity I engaged in where conflict could arise, to overcome my fear, I placed emphasis on preparation and practice. I would prepare my points and consider the individual's counter. I didn't want to make it a competition, and I was not looking to win if I were wrong. I would examine the issue close to be sure I was correct in my criticism. My objective was always to learn and grow from the session. I wanted to help a person learn and grow from the fault not destroy them over it. I wanted to hear from the subordinate and be open to having my criticism challenged. My delivery would be calm, and I would allow the subordinate to be heard. My objective would be to get them to identify the failure's causes before I did and tell me what they learned from it. I would briefly describe the failure then ask them to tell me how it happened. If they shirked responsibility, I could get more direct asking them what ownership they had in the failure. For those who could not accept fault, the session would have to end in disagreement. Failure to accept ownership of fault would now present another problem. This person may possess a flaw preventing them from serving effectively in my organization.

I always came from a good place. I was not vindictive, seeking enjoyment from admonishing someone. I always wanted what was in their best interest. I, too, failed several times and was admonished. It was hard, but I knew my boss was right. I admired his bravery, took ownership of my failures and strove to do better. It would be easier if I knew my boss was trying to invest in me. I took the same approach.

Good listener. If you don't know how to listen, the "'Investing in People' house" I mention at the beginning of this chapter will surely crumble. Listening is a characteristic you can develop. Start by thinking of people you know who are poor listeners and think about what it is they do which causes you to label them as such. I always despised the leaders who cut me off when I was answering their question or making a point or whose attention drifted away when I was talking. One of my bosses could not put down his smartphone while in a meeting. He would look at and respond to email or texts even while people were briefing him. People want to be heard. Ask probing questions and show interest.

I saw a piece by a comedian years ago comparing men and women and their listening skills. In the woman group, one of the ladies tells a story of a fender-bender she gets into on her way to the store. The ladies immediately display concern and ask if everyone was okay. In the male group, a guy tells the same story, and before he can finish, another man in the group cuts him off and describes his experience in a fender-bender when it happened to him. It's funny, especially delivered by a comedian but I see it happen all the time with both men and woman. I am genuinely fascinated by people, what they do, where they have been and what they have going on in their lives. In a counseling session, I would rather miss getting to some of my questions in order to let a subordinate tell me a personal story about something they were particularly proud of or perhaps were struggling with.

Invest some personal time in being a better listener. As much as I have studied and practiced listening, I still need improvement. Practice steps like using body language and responding to show that you are listening. Try not to put yourself in situations where you know you will be distracted. Sometimes I would reschedule counseling sessions because I knew the issue I was dealing with at that moment demanded my full attention. If I knew I could not commit to listening, I would at least tell the person talking to me and excuse myself offering another chance to talk when I could give them the attention they deserved. My advice to you; be quiet and let your people do the talking. You will be fascinated by them and they, in turn, will be grateful.

Self-Aware. Know yourself. Be consciously aware of your own character and feelings. I will cover the topic of self-awareness three times in this book; it is that important. Here, I will cover it from an organizational foundation perspective then later in Chapter 5, you will hear about my journey of becoming more self-aware. In Chapter 6, I will show you my own process for self-awareness where I break down the creation of my biography sketch. The American Management Association studied 72 executives in successful companies and found that self-awareness was the top criteria contributing to their success. The study highlighted that executives who are aware of their weaknesses are often better able to hire subordinates who perform well in categories in which the leader lacks wisdom. These leaders are also better able to entertain the possibility that someone on their team may have an idea that is even better than their own. You cannot invest in others until you invest in yourself. This does not suggest that you place your own needs above all others, rather, know who you are, the good the bad and the ugly. This will take some bravery and humility. Do you know if you are an introvert or an extrovert and what that means for how you lead and communicate? What are the five characteristics you would use to describe yourself? What are five traits? What are your strengths and weaknesses? Knowing these are important but sharing them with your team will be even more important if you care to invest in them. Do your subordinates know themselves well enough? Your people do not expect that you are without flaw and an expert at everything. You will better serve them through your self-awareness than you will attempting to be someone or something that you are not. Moreover, your people will serve you better if they know your weaknesses and how you communicate. I attended a self-awareness seminar the summer before I took command of my brigade. It contributed tremendously toward my self-awareness. I'll talk in more detail about this seminar in Chapter 5. Below, I want share two stories that illustrate the importance of self-awareness and provide you a way to start your own self-awareness journey.

Early in my career as a leader, I attempted (foolishly) to do things I was not well-equipped for. For instance, I am a horrible mechanic. I've done some basic maintaining of vehicles over the years, but maintenance was never an area of comfort for me. I could build a maintenance program, issue intent and supervise to ensure people were engaged in maintenance activities but I lacked a mechanic's expertise and intuition to diagnose and remedy problems. As a platoon leader with a small fleet of tactical vehicles, I was responsible for their maintenance. I made a fool of myself a few times trying to be a mechanic just to show my subordinates that I could do what they did. Recognizing (the hard way) that I lacked mechanical skills, I invested my time connecting with my unit's mechanics to learn about maintenance procedures. I wasn't ashamed to admit gaps in my capability. I did what basic tasks I could to show I was not afraid to get my hands dirty but I placed trust in my people. I listened to them and asked pointed questions when their answers did not make sense.

Much later in my career, well after I had taken command of my brigade, I received some of the best leadership feedback I had received in 25 years. A mentor and my boss described three people; the Visionary, the Mule and the Closer. The Visionary is one who looks big and deep and who tends to overlook small details or rushes to put a plan into action. The Mule is one who can successfully take on an enormous task load. This person can multi-task with the best of them but is more focused on the present task at hand. The Closer wraps up the project places it on "autopilot" and hits "send." This person is focused on mission or program completion in order to move on to future missions. In my career, I had performed successfully as all three when required though I preferred to be the Visionary. My comfort zone was always as a visionary. I am a strategic thinker and leader and can connect the present to the future. Because of this, I struggled getting daily directives out and driving the organization through current tasks. This didn't make me a failure as a leader. I just needed a Closer and a Mule nearby to complete me like a co-pilot would for an aircraft captain. The key was being conscious of it so I could serve my organizations best. It was important that my people knew this as well.

For your own self-awareness journey, start by taking some personality tests. You can find additional resources on the Internet. I'll provide a link to my website at the end of this chapter where I share some of the better places to gain improved self-awareness. Most importantly, do something with the data you gather from these tests. Think about what it says about you. Summarize it in a self-awareness bumper sticker or paragraph which best describes you. Document it formally. Show it to peers, superiors and subordinates and see if they agree. Show it to your family. Carry it around along with that extra voice inside you which reminds you of who you are and who you are not. Next, have your own people do this and share their results with you. It will serve you and your team extremely well.

VISION

On to ingredient number two. In the words of the Cheshire Cat, "If you don't know where you are going, any road will take you there." Vision is an essential ingredient in the foundation of investing in people. You will see mention of it several times in this book. You cannot invest in people or measure them against anything unless they are guided by a vision. Moreover, having a team of people placing everything they have behind the achievement of that vision is a powerful force. Consider an NFL football team like the New

England Patriots. Everything that team does is centered on a vision of winning the Super Bowl. Every team member in every position does his best to perform at their peak. Every coach commits himself completely to preparing players and creating plays to defeat other teams. Every member of the Patriots stands ready to sacrifice for their team to win.

As small as it might be, every organization requires a vision summarized in an organizational vision statement. Simply put, a vision is a view of a future state encapsulated in words. Many organizational vision statements are not really visions but statements of an objective such as "be the best seller," "number 1 in our market," or they describe a road-map or plan instead of an image of a future state. Susan Ward with The Balance, a business consulting firm, helps clarify a vision statement by stating what it is not. "Don't confuse a vision statement with a road map for your small business's future success; it's not. What Bill Gates envisioned when he first started Microsoft was a personal computer in every home and business, not a series of steps for making that happen." Getting it right is so essential to the success of an organization, and if you invest in your people properly, they should get behind you like the players do to the coaches of the New England Patriots. Lastly, to be effective, your vision statement should pass a set of criteria Dr. John P. Kotter outlines in *Leading Change*. It must be imaginable, desirable, feasible, focused, flexible and communicable. Hoisting the NFL's Lombardi Trophy over a celebrating team passes the Kotter test. How to get there individually and organizationally is what a team of committed players and coaches will dedicate their lives to figure out.

The Vision of 1st Brigade, 101st Airborne Division. For my brigade, our vision focused on that moment when our training, investing in people and care of families was complete, and soldiers were boarding a plane that would deliver them to a combat zone. It would be the moment the umpire yelled "Play ball!" All our preparation would be behind us. In my mind, I could picture my soldiers boarding an aircraft with serviceable combat gear tightly secured to their bodies and determined looks on their faces ready to step into harm's way in a foreign land. If we could achieve our vision, victory would be assured. In Chapter 4, you can read more about the environment I entered when I took command which greatly informed the creation of our shared vision. My brigade's vision statement: *"A disciplined, professional, physically and mentally fit Air Assault Brigade which lives the Army's Values and possesses the knowledge and skills required to succeed in any combat operation. It will be trained and ready to understand the complexities of the operational environment, iden-tify problems and their causes, tailor its structure and procedures to achieve operational objectives, and measure the effectiveness of its actions."*

I shared this vision out of a sense of duty as the book's author and to use it as a teaching point. This vision has its faults. Susan Ward and Dr. Kotter might have given me a C- if they were generous. The statement lacks focus, and it's not very communicable. You could argue that it is hard to imagine as well. The vision was too long and tried to cover everything for an organization with such a wide portfolio. It needed to be a focused statement that could be memo-rized by everyone in the brigade. We attempted to include all the words we believed were essential to our vision and should not have. Causal to its faults was an unknown future, a portfolio which was far too wide-ranging (do everything to a standard of excellence) and a schedule loaded with entirely too many non-combat focused events. If we were a profit-driven, private organization, we might have failed by taking on so much and trying to prepare for the unknown. But because we were a government funded organization, manned by volunteers serving a cause indoctrinated with Army values and culture, we could overcome and produce a relevant organization. For this, I credit my leaders. These leaders, co-authors of our vision, championed it in everything they did translating it to soldiers and connecting all our combat preparation to our imagined future. Our vision appeared on every counseling statement I used and in every introductory meeting I held with anyone new to the team. This, along with establishing priorities, helped us overcome a more focused and communicable vision statement.

If I were to rewrite it today, it would look closer to this. *We are the Army's most ready and relevant warriors who will win on today's complex battlefield.* This vision summarizes the larger statement above. Ready includes the professional, physical and discipline requirements of a combat unit. Relevant speaks to our modern approaches against asymmetric threats which require innovative plans and operations and organizational changes in order to defeat them. Win promotes the confidence in the organization as it steps off to combat; we will win. Lastly, the complex battlefield describes an environment ranging widely between lethal action to kill or capture enemies and non-lethal actions to engage with indigenous populations to learn about grievances and issues which are causal to the creation of these enemies.

While your vision statement should stand alone and meet the Kotter criteria, you can complement it with values and organizational culture in subsequent sentences to further promote who you are and what is important to you as an organization. Values and culture are codependent. Culture consists of shared values in an organization. For example, a tech company like Apple must establish and foster a culture of innovation. Innovation is in its company vision statement. To support this culture of innovation, its people must possess values like creativity and courage to explore the unknown and impossible. Apple employees who embrace deliberate and formal experimentation and vetting and approval processes will be obstacles standing in the way of vision achievement. To understand both values and culture, I'll dissect them separately below.

Organizational values. John Coleman, an author and contributor to *Harvard Business Review* and *Forbes*, states, "A company's values are the core of its culture ... and offer a set of guidelines on the behaviors and mindsets needed to achieve that vision." In the Army, we have a core set of values that soldiers learn and pledge to uphold in their initial entry training and education. They are Loyalty, Duty, Respect, Selfless Service, Honor, Integrity and Personal Courage. When a soldier does wrong, regardless of rank, it can almost always be traced to a violation of one or more of these core values. For instance, if one soldier were to sexually assault another, they would be violating every one of the Army's values in some way. They are excellent, and I was fortunate that the Army did that work for me. We embodied them in our vision and in our daily work.

You could easily emulate the Army Values with a set of values of your own. In a diverse group of organizational members, list out as many values as possible. Keep your list inside you while you let others contribute first. Once you have values listed out for all to see, pick the ones you think best describe the people of your organization. Keep chipping away until you agree on a small list. Once complete, spend time defining each one and how it relates to your organization. Provide examples or vignettes of people espousing and violating these values to ensure understanding. Along with the vision statement, formally distribute these organizational values to your team. Hire and develop people who subscribe to these values and hold accountable anyone who violates them.

Organizational culture. Study.com defines organizational culture as "a system of shared assumptions, values, and beliefs, which governs how people behave in organizations." In the Army, a soldier's behavior could be described as selfless. Soldiers are always concerned about their buddy and sacrifice themselves for the betterment of their buddies. For shared assumptions, the Army and its soldiers subscribe to the Warrior Ethos. The Warrior Ethos defines a culture of men and women who put the mission first and always place their buddy's needs before their own. The ethos states: "I will always place the mission first. I will never accept defeat. I will never quit, and I will never leave a fallen comrade." When a leader in the Army sees a soldier, he can safely assume that no matter the task, they will never quit or let their buddies down. Their belief is that it's all about a team and not themselves individually. It's a set of predictive behavior allowing the Army to take on the toughest missions anywhere in the world. This ethos helped me and my organization overcome a lofty, lengthy vision statement.

In a start-up tech company, its culture may be defined by people who will not stop at the first technical challenge, who will embrace the innovative spirit and the unknown in a quest for a better, more efficient way. A player on the New England Patriots in a team-first culture knows it is not about his personal statistics, rather how he can help the player next to him be better.

How to create your vision. Vision creation is a complex process especially the larger and more diverse the organization. I've provided a link to my website at the end of this chapter where I outline the steps I took when building mine. It starts with establishing an environment where leaders can assemble free of distractions to think and create. It is then followed by forming the right team of diverse and divergent thinkers and leaders. Once the team is set, spend ample time polling the group to define or frame the current environment (markets, existing organizational problems, government regulation, etc.). Dedicate a preponderance of your time to understanding the environment before you commit to drafting a vision statement. Once you feel that everyone has a good grasp of internal and external descriptors that define your environment you are ready for the next step. Sketch out the first draft of the vision with team input then release the group. Reassemble days later, collect team input, run the Kotter test then develop your vision's final version. Here, you can discuss a vision implementation strategy following the Kotter 8-Step model to promote the new vision. Beta test the vision statement with employees and collect feedback.

For your preparation, I highly suggest you watch a TED Talk by Simon Sinek titled "How Great Leaders Inspire Action." It is simply the best 18-minute education on the "why" instead of the "what" behind organizations. In the talk, Sinek posits, the power behind a successful vision is to get people to believe what you believe in. He cites a few examples illustrating his point. Study successful visions and examine why they've succeeded. Finally, invest in the employees charged to carry it out.

PRIORITIES

Last ingredient. Amidst an environment overwhelmed by information and task loads, you will not be able to invest in your people unless you establish and enforce priorities. If everything is a priority, nothing is a priority. Most organizations have more to do than they have time for. If you have the power to lighten the task load, then you should but if not, establish priorities. You are not serving your people if you dole out a monstrous list of tasks without prioritization or guidance to help them. My soldiers and leaders wanted my help handling an enormous task load. Establishing priorities was the most effective way. I did my best to rank order priorities, but where I couldn't, I placed trust in my leaders to prioritize in accordance with our shared vision. This wasn't a "good luck" approach. My senior leaders and I invested ample time reviewing daily priorities as established by junior leaders to ensure vision alignment. We would coach subordinates along if they were off the mark and provide space and resources as required to help them operate. I knew that by investing in them, as I have described in this book, they would rise to the occasion. They could always ask questions and often did. Along with daily priorities, you should establish a set of enduring priorities to guide your teams in times of ambiguity. These are priorities which will remain regardless of changing conditions. For example, I knew investing in people would be an enduring priority for my organization. Physical training (PT) would be as well. Leaders needed to have very good reason to cancel PT. I trusted them to make that call, but they always knew it was an enduring priority. Like PT, I never took investing in people off the list. For those tasks that fell in the lower priority category, I could assume risk meaning if they were not accomplished we would still survive the day. For instance, if Friday was the day for our monthly arms room inventory, but soldiers were returning to their unit area late due to a PT event, we could slide the inventory to the following Monday to give PT the priority.

Your employees need daily and enduring priorities as well and the power to make adjustments in accordance with these priorities and your organizational vision. They may have to shift priorities on their own based on conditions. For instance, if the stated priority for the day is the preparation of product X for delivery and a customer calls with a complaint not related to this priority, then the priority for that individual shifts from product X to the customer's needs.

Risk is an important component of prioritization. It's not easy or possible in many cases to say that you will ignore a task. As an example, I could never issue guidance stating that a deadline was to be disregarded. I could ask for extensions or challenge a certain directive, but most of the time I would have to live with what my headquarters sent to me. I would focus instead on priorities. Think about the product X story. In that case, the priority for the day was preparation of product X for delivery. However, customer service was an enduring priority that took precedence. At the end of the day, if product X was not ready for shipment, this risk might be more acceptable than losing a customer and ruining a good company reputation. In my two years in command, we accomplished numerous large-scale events. One of them was a large-scale move of unit headquarters, barracks and maintenance facilities from one end of the Army post to another. My guidance for this mission started with people. I was not going to assume any risk in caring for people. I would not accept a substandard environment for my soldiers such as moving into a barracks that was not suitable or a facility that might cause a leader to lose his or her assigned equipment. I didn't ignore designated tasks and deadlines, but I did tell my team I would accept risk on these requirements before placing a soldier in a substandard room.

Closing. The point of this chapter was to prevent the rush to failure. Establish your foundation first. Take some quality time to get yourself, your organizational vision and priorities established, so the foundation is solid. This foundation is a journey and not something done in an afternoon. This will allow you to move forward with your investment in people. You do not have to build this foundation alone. Aside from some self-reflection, seek the help and wisdom of others on your team to establish the best foundation you can. Share drafts of your work with your people and seek their feedback before building your house. Make it about them. After all, it's personal, not personnel.

Visit *www.RobCampbellLeadership.com/Book*, where I share products to assist you with vision creation, leading change and self-awareness.

Chapter 5
MY STORY ABOUT INVESTING IN PEOPLE, AND HOW YOU CAN CREATE YOUR OWN

I have been leading by investing in people throughout my career. I have almost always given of my time, talent and experience for the betterment of others. As a young officer, I remember a mentor of mine always talking about making a difference in those around him, one person at a time. That resonated with me and I always took that approach in the countless organizations I led. Where I might have gotten lazy and not addressed a deficit in another or where I may not have known a subordinate and his or her family as well as I should, I saw the negative results. I was unable to appraise them appropriately, or I missed an opportunity or failed in my duty to help them advance in their career. I paid the price or better said; they paid the price for my lack of investment. The command of an Army brigade would be leadership at a scale I had not experienced before. The gravity of the command forced me to reflect on my leadership more than I had before. It forced me to codify it under a banner like

"Investing in People" and carry it and my approaches into this vast organization. Here is the story of that journey.

MY COMMAND SELECTION AND THE ENVIRONMENT IN THE FALL OF 2013

I was promoted to the rank of Colonel in April of 2012. It was a humbling promotion, especially because the selection rate was only 33 percent. Following selection for promotion, the Army selects a subset of the promoted population to command or serve as the commander or CEO of a brigade (3,000-5,000 soldiers and their families.) I competed for this selection and was picked to command the 1st Brigade of the famed 101st Airborne Division. The news humbled me beyond words. I was to be the leader of an organization just shy of 5,000 soldiers; deployable worldwide to fight our nation's wars like it had done in World War II, Vietnam, Desert Storm and Iraq and Afghanistan. I would follow in the footsteps of some of the Army's most legendary leaders, people I'd marveled over my entire career. My job would be to educate and train soldiers for combat ensuring they had the equipment and supplies they needed. I would be responsible for the successes and failures of the organization and for the care of its soldiers and their families. Aside from being a husband and father, it was the honor of my life.

I was to take command of the brigade in the fall of 2013. During this period, the Army was catching its breath having only recently closed out an 8-year war in Iraq and during the winding down our involvement in Afghanistan. At that time, there was talk by the president and his cabinet of the Afghanistan war coming to an end. This would impact my command tenure as we were scheduled to deploy there in 2014. In the fall of 2013, the Army was struggling with several social and behavioral issues, some which were a result of years of sustained combat. While suicide rates were down slightly from 2012, they remained at a 5-year high and had bypassed combat deaths prior to my taking command. Sexual harassment had also surfaced as a military-wide problem gaining Congressional and Army senior leadership attention. Along with these, combat stress, family separation from repeat deployments, marital and relationship failures and abuse and off-duty misconduct like driving intoxicated all proved to be a significant challenge for leaders at all levels. The Army was struggling to build resilience in its soldiers, and many lacked coping skills to overcome these personal and family challenges. Add to all this the ambiguous future the brigade was facing. Having just returned from a 12-month deployment to Afghanistan prior to my assuming command, the soldiers in the brigade, as well as their families, were wondering if we were headed back as scheduled or if the deployment would be canceled altogether. If not Afghanistan, would the brigade be headed to another distant land? It was a period of increased angst for the Army and 1st Brigade of the 101st Airborne Division. Talk about an environment ripe for investing in people. This was the Super Bowl!

COMMAND PREPARATION

Fortunately, during the summer before I took command, I attended a series of command preparation courses where I took time to think and prepare. One above all was of particular value. The Army sent me to a seminar called the True Growth Academy focused on producing authentic, introspective leaders. This seminar, which helped me understand and define my character and calling had a lasting impact on me. As a selfless leader throughout my career, aside from a few personality tests, I never invested time reflecting on who I was and my life's core purpose. I was always busy serving others. This seminar provided that much-needed opportunity. It was a period of tremendous personal reflection and learning. There, I was able to participate in a 360-degree survey where my peers, superiors and subordinates provided an assessment of my personality and leadership. I was able to see how people perceived me as a leader, what they appreciated most and what they thought I could improve on. I did my own assessment prior to seeing the results and compared how I saw myself against how others saw me. Among several compliments, I was criticized for my lack of patience and occasional periods where people found me deep in thought oblivious to those around me. That criticism was particularly valuable. I could recall times when I was probably mulling over an issue in my head, and I am sure that those around me were wondering where I was. I did tend to bottle issues up a bit and knew I needed to work on that. This feedback was fair and helpful.

In the two-day seminar, I determined my interpersonal style and chose from a collection of values and leadership behaviors I believed were most important. In the 25 years, I had served prior to the seminar; I had never done this. I found it indispensable to my desires to invest in the people of my brigade. If we were to connect with each other and serve together during trying times, we would need to be self-aware, authentic leaders. That would start with me, and I was grateful for this timely dose of training. About a year into my tenure, I brought the seminar to my organization to help my leaders with introspection and authenticity. They raved about it and to this day, many still recall what a positive impact it had on them as leaders and people. It helped me tremendously connect to my people. There are a number of self-development or awareness seminars available to organizations, and I would highly recommend choosing one to best fit your needs. They will make a difference for your team. Later, I will share one the most important outcomes of my self-awareness journey, my core purpose.

While at one of the command preparation courses that summer, I was out with friends having a drink and of course, like a group of leaders, we shared our experiences in leadership and command. That night, I was introduced to Tim Leroux, a recently retired Army officer. We began talking about counseling, and he gave me an idea which I readily stole, put into practice and still use today. Tim served as a professor of military science for the officer's training program (ROTC) at the local college before his retirement from the Army. While there, he directed his officer candidates to produce their biography (BIO) sketch. In the Army, a BIO is like a resume. It provides a chronological listing of unit assignments, certifications, awards and lists family members. These standard BIOs, while helpful to see where a soldier served and what he or she possesses for qualifications, actually say little about the person. The BIO sketches he had his candidates produce focused on them personally. These sketches highlighted where they'd worked in high school, what their childhood passions were, how they saw their weaknesses and strengths, what their personal and professional goals were and how they wanted to be remembered after they departed each assignment. This sunk in. Given the environment I was about to step into, I thought this would be particularly relevant. If I could let my guard down and show my soldiers and their families that I was a human like them shaped by my passions, regrets, strengths and weaknesses and life experiences it could have a big impact. Additionally, in requiring BIO sketches from my leaders, I could learn a great deal which would help me invest in them. I had authored several important organizational policies and professional papers in my career. My BIO sketch would be one of my most important. Here is a portion of it. You can view the complete sketch on my website.

MY BIOGRAPHY SKETCH

• •

Colonel Rob Campbell
October 2013

I joined the Army in 1987 during my freshman year in college. I found myself short of money like many college students, and the college benefits the Massachusetts Army National Guard were offering seemed very attractive. So, I decided to enlist. It was not out of a sense of duty or patriotism, though I did want to be like my dad who had served in the Army Reserves. If you would have told me in high school that I was to be a career Army officer I would have laughed at you. It was never a passion or dream of mine. Once in the National Guard, I found ROTC in college and quickly grew fond of the leadership challenges and soldiering. Soon it became my infatuation, and I desired a career as an Army officer after graduation.

I grew up in Massachusetts with my three sisters in the same town and enjoyed basketball and motorcycle riding. These were my passions growing up, and motorcycle riding remains so. I was the class clown, smart-ass and family comedian. I worked as a landscaper and at a department store in the hardware department during my high school and college years. I am a proud "Yankee" and a big fan of all New England sports.

I was never selected ahead of my peers for promotion or expected I would be chosen for command. My family and I have learned to take the Army one assignment at a time at this stage of my career. Regardless of how far my Army career goes, I will walk away with a great sense of satisfaction and gratitude over what the Army has given me.

Like others, I am a man shaped by my life experiences, personally and professionally. I have two sons, one in college and one in high school. I married my high school sweetheart and have been with her for 22 years. The love of my immediate family is what keeps me going each day. I enjoy being with them and cherish a life of great memories in places the Army sent us. We love it here at Fort Campbell.

My father died of cancer in June of 2012, and my relationship with some members of my immediate family took a turn. They say that a crisis can bring out the worst in people. There were some behaviors toward my wife and I that were unforgivable, unrepairable and that would eventually impact our marriage and health. Because of this, we severed ties with them. This life-changing experience made me a more authentic person and has strengthened my marriage and relationship with my immediate family. We have excluded them from our lives and have focused on what is important: our health and well-being.

My experiences in combat in Iraq and Afghanistan had significant impact on me personally and professionally. It was these assignments which shaped my view of modern warfare. We must place better emphasis on understanding the environments we are deployed to and tailor our organizations and processes to address core problems and understand population failings. It's not as simple as killing our way toward a solution. I believe there is great change required in defense and in US government policy if we are to achieve success addressing terrorism.

I believe my strengths are strong leadership qualities, selflessness, compassion and humility. Like many leaders, I have an ego but do not let it get the best of me. I believe that I listen and place trust in those around me. I am not as quick to understand an issue as I would like to be. I am a commander that needs a staff. I suffer from ADD though not acutely. It does impact my concentration, and I have trouble sometimes getting started on something. Though capable, I don't like to make an immediate decision. I've been criticized for this. I like to see the work and analysis behind a problem before I decide. I like group versus individual think. My strange sense of humor can be misinterpreted at times, so I have to be more aware of my surroundings, what I say and what I do.

After I am gone, I want to be remembered as someone who invested in people, challenged them to be better and more authentic, who showed compassion and understanding, and who made a difference in the lives of others. My life's core purpose is to make a difference in the lives of others through optimistic leadership.

I scored ENTP on the Myers-Briggs Type Indicator. The ENTP has been described as the innovator, the originator, the lawyer, the inventor, the explorer, and the visionary. My interpersonal style can be explained as Expressive: Fast-paced. Outgoing. Enthusiastic. Tends to be guided more by vision than by facts. Establishes open, trusting relationships. Collaborates in finding and implementing quality solutions. Sees the big picture before probing for details. Futuristic. Holistic thinker. Inspiring. Direct and open. Energetic. Gestures that are open and wide. Voice that is loud and varied. Lively.

• •

TAKING CHARGE

Summer of 2013 ended, and the Army did its job preparing me for the most important assignment of my career. I was going to put the "personal" into my "personnel." It would be the organization's top priority amidst what was to be an extremely eventful two-year tour. To support this priority, I would need to back it up with some people-centric leadership philosophies. I've listed them below.

- Do only those things that only I can do

- Listen and learn

- Lead change

Do only those things that only I can do. A mentor of mine introduced me to this philosophy, and I watched him live by it, undistracted by numerous demands, many of which other people in his charge could address. I had done many of the jobs which exist in an Army brigade. I didn't need to do them again. Only I could counsel and develop my battalion (a sub-organization consisting of 400-700 soldiers and family members) commanders. Only I could finalize and personally send the weekly update to my boss highlighting the brigade's activities. Only I could select the future leaders of the Army and communicate this to HRC through efficiency reports and personal phone calls. Only I could chair and direct our monthly soldiers of concern and family readiness steering group. Others in my organization could run the brigade guided by my intent ensuring property was accounted for, soldiers were housed and fed, training was resourced and equipment was maintained. Of course, I would provide my intent to ensure these were done to standard. There would be some risk with this approach as I would not always have the pulse of the organization. However, my staff and subordinate leaders were equipped with my intent and information requirements, and I trusted them to notify me of anything deserving my attention. This philosophy allowed me to look deep and think big which I needed to do. Most importantly, it allowed me to spend time with my people.

Listen and learn. The previous summer I had drafted my vision and intent for the brigade, but that was done in a vacuum away from a living and breathing organization. I left it on my hard drive. I wasn't aware how well the brigade was investing in its people prior to my arrival. I didn't know what good things the brigade was already doing and where a stronger people-focus was needed. I was taking over a brigade that had just returned from a combat tour conducting security force assistance (SFA), training and advising Afghan National Security Forces. I had not deployed for three years by the time I took command. There were leaders and soldiers in the organization fresh from the battlefield whose combat relevance exceeded mine. I was okay with that. They were proud of their recent accomplishments and wanted to do more of the same in the coming year. While proud of their recent successes, the future was largely unknown, and I knew I had to prepare the brigade for a wide variety of missions instead of the narrow SFA capability. I had to hear from the leaders of the organization to gauge this and determine our start point. I had to determine how my leaders understood warfare and how they saw our role in it. Did they see it like I did? Did I have it right? It would have been easy building on the brigade's newly gained SFA proficiency, but we were missing an SFA mandate. I wasn't sure where we might be called to action and for what. Along with determining people and combat focus, I needed to listen to leaders and soldiers across the brigade to understand how we did business. There were established standard operating procedures (SOPs) in the organization, some different than what I was used to and I needed to hear about them so I could either adapt and follow or change them. The key to this discovery was taking formal briefs from my subordinate organizations that displayed their combat readiness status, current issues and who their leadership teams were. Coupled with this formal series of briefings, I set about having numerous informal discussions with soldiers and leaders across the organization to ask questions about the topics above and to seek their suggestions for the future.

Lead change. The ambiguity of our future coupled with the social issues of 2013, necessitated that I lead change. Along with this, I was a different leader from my predecessor, not better or worse, just different. He happened to be a friend of mine and handed over a very good unit. Along with my arrival, five of my subordinate commanders were new to the team. This wholesale leadership reappointment would most certainly bring change to the unit, and I had to lead it and get the existing members to embrace it. People are resistant to change, so I had to subscribe to a formal change model if I wanted to succeed. I chose the Dr. John P. Kotter 8-Step Leading Change model, specifically "Build a Guiding Coalition" (my battalion commanders) and "Enlist a Volunteer Army" (my company commanders.) I've included this process for you on my website and urge you to study it further. Aside from new personalities, this change would consist of afresh emphasis on people and a focus on core land warfare competency education and training over SFA. For education and training, the brigade was in full SFA mindset, and many wanted to stay there. However, ambiguity would require us to return to a common core. Once we gained mission clarity, we could adjust from that point to educate and train against stated objectives. Guided by our new brigade-shared vision, my team would build an innovative and relevant education and training program for land warfare. Changes to how I and my leaders would invest in our people would help bring that program to reality.

People would get us through this, not computers or weapons or helicopters. I believed that if I took care of my people if I could show them that I was human and vulnerable like them, if they knew I considered their well-being and personal growth my mission, everyone would step up and do the right thing. If I built that trust between us, they would perform no matter the task. Because investing in people was the priority, I had to personally demonstrate it. Words alone would not suffice. I did this by verbalizing its importance repeatedly, monitoring and inspecting execution, managing my time in conjunction with this priority and by personally managing the careers of my leaders. Here is my Investing in People "To Do" list prior to taking command. It's not in order of priority. That changed based on the evolving environment. I'll expand on these in the pages ahead and tell you what you can do to replicate it.

INVESTING IN PEOPLE "TO DO" LIST

- Investing in People events reflected by my personal calendar
- Personally select random soldier counseling packets for review and assessment
- Meet early with my HR manager to set tone and explain my intent
- Visit and question leaders to test their understanding of our #1 priority
- Champion deserving leaders by communicating with their personnel managers at HRC
- Adopt and grow the Soldiers of Concern Program
- Get out of my office and visit soldiers and leaders
- Conduct sensing sessions with sample populations across the brigade to obtain and maintain the pulse of the organization
- Send personal notes to soldiers and distant family members
- Send notes to my leaders on their anniversaries and birthdays
- Establish and foster a strong family support and readiness program
- Measure the effectiveness of our efforts

My calendar. A mentor of mine told me that my priorities would be reflected in my shared calendar for everyone to view. This would advertise what I thought was important. I took heed of that counsel. I was not going to pay lip-service to investing in people and calendar management in accordance with this priority was one way to demonstrate this. I demanded that one-third of my calendar be filled with counseling. Even while deployed to Afghanistan, with a portion of my brigade back home I would video teleconference with individuals for one-hour counseling sessions. Many of the "To Do" list items you see above were events on my calendar. I spoke earlier of prioritization. That was the name of the game when it came to building and managing my calendar. We had a standard schedule we called our battle rhythm. This was a uniform set of reoccurring events like meetings, briefings and in-progress reviews which were synchronized and fed a decision cycle for myself and information requirements from my higher headquarters. Along with counseling, I prioritized battle rhythm events related to investing in people such as our Soldiers of Concern program and sensing sessions. I booked time early and often for my brigade HR officer (called the S1 in an Army brigade) and his deputy to review progress and give guidance. It was not easy balancing all my personal requirements, however; I was passionate about investing in people. I didn't have to fake it with calendar events. I wanted these events on my calendar for all the right reasons, and my organization knew this. The message was clear, and I could not have done it without calendar management.

What you can do. Whether you know it or not, you probably have a battle rhythm in your own organization. This rhythm probably feeds decisions for the boss or reviews recent or upcoming sales and periods and productivity indicators. Make your own "To Do" list and reflect it on your calendar. Color code events by category like blue for instance, for events that are people-centric. Share your calendar. Personally, live by a set of priorities for when events collide and ensure your staff or assistant knows this. For instance, I would take our monthly Soldiers of Concern meeting over a staff update if the two were to collide as I know I could have more positive influence that way. You can also publish some enduring guidance for your calendar to all your organizational members, so they know what is important to you. I didn't do this formally but wish that I had. This approach will keep you on task and broadcast to your organization the importance of investing in people. Visit the HR department often and give them a seat at the table in your calendar events as I did by providing them a voice in my daily morning huddle. Meet with your people formally and informally but carve time out in your calendar for this. If you do not, you will be consumed by the crisis of the moment or some other distractor. You can have others help you invest in your people, but you cannot delegate the task.

Inspect counseling (or employee performance reviews.) Word went out like wildfire when leaders learned that I was hand-picking counseling packets. I would use a generic organizational manning document and ask my subordinate leaders to personally retrieve counseling packets from the positions I selected. This prevented someone from cherry-picking the best ones from their unit. I would have these personally delivered, and I would hold them securely in my office. I would review them for administrative data and review other forms that were in the folder but would spend a preponderance of my time looking at the performance counseling forms. Some packets were very immature meaning the counselor and counselee had only been recently assigned to each other. In these cases, my focus was on the initial counseling. I examined it to see if a set of standards had been outlined and if the counselor had highlighted his or her expectations. No soldier was to exist in the brigade without fully understanding what was expected of them. In more mature packets, I saw a pattern of counseling statements. Some of these packets were done well, meaning they described strengths and weaknesses of the counselee, challenged the counselee to improve and offered techniques to do so. Many unfortunately were very dry and ineffective. They might only discuss what the unit was doing or offer simple challenges like improving marksmanship or physical fitness scores. These packets left out the essential part of counseling which was to focus on weaknesses of the soldier and how he or she could overcome them. I shared the packets with my CSM because of his wealth of experience. I would then contact the commander of that organization to give him or her my review. This was a lengthy process, and I didn't collect counseling as often as I would have liked, but it did result in improvements.

What you can do. First, you should ensure your leaders are prepared to counsel people. I always started any effort determining the capability of my people. If they are not, train them or hire an outside agency to train your leaders on how to conduct developmental performance counseling, mentoring or coaching, whichever term your organization uses. Start by establishing standards and expectations for counseling such as how often you want it conducted and what outcomes you expect. A review and discussion of personal and professional goals and strengths and weaknesses could be a one-directed outcome to force the conversation. Issue clear intent for everyone to understand and achieve as they build and execute the program. Once started, ensure that counseling or performance reviews are being conducted. Doers do what checkers check. If your team knows that you will be inspecting, however you choose to do it, they will likely step up their game. You should attempt to review the strengths and weaknesses of your subordinates as well as their performance. When reviewing these forms, ask yourself if the counseling or appraisal is what you would like to receive or if you believe it would help you improve and grow. Ask yourself if the counseling or appraisal really accomplishes what it should; the review of the positives and negatives of a person and how they should work to improve the negatives. Ask yourself if the counseling or appraisal is a wise investment of time.

My Brigade S1. My S1 or Human Resource Officer was the first staff officer I met with. I had nine staff sections in the brigade. His was the first and most frequent one I met with. Other staff members got their share of my attention, and some needed me more than others, but the S1 would be my enduring priority. In our first meeting, I had a chance to describe much of what I have written about in this book and offer my help. I made my people-centric priority perfectly clear. I told him he would have a seat at the table in my most important meetings and that he had direct access to me.

Knowing of a few performance standards I saw lacking in this unit and many I had served in previously, I gave him some early guidance. I instructed him and his deputy that I wanted zero late efficiency report submissions. I would not tolerate efficiency reports done last minute missing the submission timeline to HRC. I saw this as a careless act by the rating officer. No, I wanted each of these reports done in advance and delivered to the rated individual formally. I had grown up in environments where people received their report by email or by the personnel manager instead of their rater. I found this impersonal and irresponsible and it was not to happen in our organization. I directed him to draft a brigade policy outlining efficiency report submission requirements (exceeding Army standards) for my signature and to keep me informed of compliance.

Next, I didn't want any deserving person in the brigade to depart without an award, formally presented in front of his or her team. My soldiers worked incredibly hard, and we placed a ton of work and responsibility on their shoulders. Unless they had engaged in misconduct, they were to be recognized as they departed the brigade. They were not to receive their award in the mail upon arrival to their next unit or after separation from the Army which I had seen happen one too many times in the past. I told him and his deputy I wanted to be number one in the division (of six other brigades) in human resource performance. This was a series of measured indicators such as medical readiness, available soldiers for deployment, efficiency report submission timeliness, legal cases, etc. I knew this was a tall order and I knew I needed to put the "A Team" on the task. He would need the help of myself and my senior enlisted noncommissioned officer, my CSM. I knew if anyone could help get us past the goal-line, it was my CSM due to his leadership and organizational behavior and efficiency experience. I stressed all this guidance to my leaders for compliance, but my HR officer and his deputy were to be my advocates or ambassadors and let me know if the organization was straying away from this priority. Unfortunately, in less than one year, because of his lack of performance, that officer would be relieved and replaced by another one who took this guidance sprinting and exceeded my expectations. I couldn't and wouldn't fire everyone who was slow to deliver results, but this was an area where I was not going to assume risk. My attempts to correct and re-train him failed. I would have moved one of my best non-HR officers into the position to help achieve my intent if that is what it took. It was that important to me. In previous assignments, I had spent too much of my personal time trying to train a substandard HR officer. That approach came at a cost, and I was not to make that mistake again.

What you can do. In a brigade of 5,000 soldiers, I had to lead at an executive or CEO level through my subordinate leaders. For me, it was my six subordinate battalion commanders and my brigade staff. My S1 did not possess authority to direct units, but she could help broadcast my intent and priorities and give me feedback. You can do the same with your HR manager or perhaps chief operations officer. However you decide to conduct an investing-in-people effort, pick a lead agent or ambassador similar to my S1 who wakes each day thinking of people and of your intent and who champions the effort. Give them some well-crafted intent. Give your HR professional any additional help like a chief operations officer or a person with authority and influence in your organization. Put your "A Team" on it. Ensure your HR section or department is sufficient enough in size for this priority. If you must outsource, do so only under strict intent and vision and ensure those outsourced live by it.

Pick a good HR professional or what I liked to call a "fire and forget" person, meaning, comparable to a smart missile that you fire it and it finds the target without your constant guidance and direction. Lend them your ear and your backing as often as you can. Establish policies which prevent situations such as late appraisals or recognition. Schedule frequent briefings like appraisal performance, administrative personnel action performance, recruitment and training and development (to name a few) that let you know you are achieving effects.

Leader visits. I engaged frequently with leaders in both formal and informal ways. In both settings, I was able to query leaders as to their knowledge and activity investing in people. Battle rhythm events were always a good catalyst for this, but I found that informal and unannounced visits were the best indicator to see if my priorities were being met. I would make attempts to see them in their own environment, around their own people. This would give me a perfect opportunity to deliver my intent in person. An old boss of mine once said: "If you want something done right once, you have to say it 10 times." I became repetitive but needed to be as a large organizational leader.

Whenever I spoke to groups of leaders and soldiers in my brigade, I would ask them to tell me the organization's number one priority.

In the early days, I had to help them with this answer. Soon it took hold all on its own and I would always hear "investing in people." My one-on-one engagement with leaders were great opportunities to tell my "machine gun" analogy or ask about a data point from their organization like late efficiency reports or substandard counseling performance or even a positive data point I may have just learned about. I could even use the opportunity to ask how they were doing personally and professionally. It might lead to more one-on-one time which I was always willing to do.

What you can do. Visit your leaders and people often and in an unannounced fashion. See them in different situations and environments. Visit them in their office and in social settings like the cafeteria. You will learn amazing things. See them in their place of duty and strike up a conversation. Use these events to broadcast your intent. Go prepared with stories and soundbites that people can remember which reinforce your priorities. Take notes; offer more one-on-one time. There is nothing like the boss's presence in the work place especially if your intent is the betterment of your people. Create events that help you engage with leaders. I had lunch with my battalion commanders each Thursday. I would schedule physical fitness followed by breakfast off the base where we could exercise in our non-military gear, get a big breakfast and talk about a variety of things. Get creative and get personal.

Champion deserving soldiers. I often communicated with HRC about a specific officer or NCO. HRC consisted of several branches that managed the varying occupational skills. In one case, I had a signal officer who was accepted to a career-enhancing school, the timing of which would have a major impact on an upcoming multi-million-dollar, brigade signal-equipment fielding and training event. I called Army Signal Branch at HRC and talked to his assignment officer. Oddly enough, I was told that I could hold him back a year. When I asked if he would be able to attend the following year's course, they could not promise that. I could not believe my ears. This HR professional was offering me an option to put this officer's career at risk. By not attending the course, that is exactly what would have happened. I sent the officer. It hurt. In an instant, our mission receiving and integrating the signal equipment became all the harder. For me, though it was painful, the answer was clear. We would find a way to rise to the occasion without him. He was an exceptional officer and deserved the opportunity. It was my duty to champion him.

Later in my tenure, I would call HRC out of the blue just to highlight the success of one or more of my officers. This would move their name up on a smaller list of exceptional officers so their branch manager could earmark them for career-enhancing assignments. Sometimes, I had rock star officers who had not yet received an efficiency report. These reports were typically the only indicator at HRC of an officer's potential. With a phone call, I could elevate a deserving officer. It could make the difference between promotion and command selection in a competitive Army. I wish I had started this initiative earlier.

What you can do. Champion your people using whatever means you have. Get to know them of course, but in addition, talk them up. Make a list of those people in your organization today who are the future leaders in your field. Identify the future COOs and CEOs. Talk to their supervisors about their advancement. Invest some education and training to grow them. If they deserve to but cannot advance in your organization, release them to another organization where they can. Use your network to endorse this person and connect them to others. Send an email to your boss explaining the great performance of one of your people. Blog about them on professional websites such as LinkedIn.com. I spoke to one HR professional who informed me that her company would talk to other similar companies to promote people. Some would view this as risky, communicating with a competitor about talented people but she told me on top of helping a person, it assisted greatly with the reputation of her organization. People who had worked in her company and had since departed to advance elsewhere endorsed her company amongst peers and on professional job search sites like GlassDoor.com.

Soldiers of Concern. I assumed a fantastic program called Soldiers of Concern (SOC) from my predecessor. SOC was a forum of subordinate commanders and my organic behavioral health, family life, family readiness and religious leaders who reviewed the cases of soldiers experiencing a wide variety of problems (financial, marriage, suicidal, misconduct, etc.). We would assemble quarterly, review the progress or decline in each of these soldiers and discuss new additions. Commanders were afforded the opportunity to receive immediate counsel from the specialists in the room. All of us learned together and worked as a team helping soldiers overcome their problems. I learned a great deal in each session and passed on my personal experience to these young leaders to help them help their soldiers and their families.

One of the things I found in these sessions was that commanders believed the fewer people they had on their list, the more successful they were. I saw it differently. More names on the list meant that commanders were busy getting to know and help their people. It was not, as some believed, an indicator of poor leadership. I saw it as a leader who was engaged with his or her soldiers. I wasn't trying to create a brigade's worth of social scientists. Most of these leaders had little training in behavioral health and the like, but they were educated men and women and experienced leaders who possessed the capability of either helping or knowing where to get help for their people. The meeting ran long, and it took leaders away from demanding requirements, but it was important. I took the program and re-emphasized it. For example, instead of the deputy commander chairing the meeting, I personally took over as I saw it vital to my investing in people efforts. We helped soldiers and leaders live better lives and may have saved a life or two in the process.

What you can do. I recognize outside of a military unit; this may be a difficult program to replicate. If you can do it, even in part, then you should. If you cannot, invest some time educating and training your leaders to identify personal conflict and agencies that can help. If you can assemble with subordinate leaders and review those people who may be experiencing hardship you might be able to assist with time off or another form of compensation or assistance. You could do this even without names involved. If you knew generically what issues your people were facing, at least you would be able to lead your organization better. If privacy and confidentially prevent this, stick to getting to know your people as best you can. You might even be able to create an informal list of people you are concerned about just by talking to leaders and their subordinates.

Getting out and visiting soldiers and family. I enjoyed getting up from behind my desk and email to walk the brigade area. At random, I would visit units, leaders, individuals, stop by barracks and eat in my own dining facility. These were great moments where I discovered the most. I could ask individuals if they had been formally counseled, get a sense of their job fulfillment and hear from them on a variety of issues. There was no genius behind this idea, but I had seen few leaders do it. I found this of enormous value and made it an informal, routine behavior of mine. Whenever I sat in my office for extended periods of time, I would grow uncomfortable wondering what person I could help and what I might learn. Each time, I would try to head in a different direction to get to as many areas and people as possible.

My wife and I visited family events as often as we could. These were
great opportunities to connect with the people who supported
my soldiers. I felt in debt to them and wanted to meet as many as
I could. During ceremonies where we would recognize individuals,
I would always seek out family members who had traveled from
out of town to be there. Consider the angst of a family surrounded
by clean-shaven warriors standing rigidly in parade formation with
sergeants barking commands. I knew for many of them this would
be uncomfortable so I saw it as my duty to connect with them as
a person and make them feel relaxed and welcomed. I also saw it as
an opportunity to thank them for providing their son or daughter
to serve with us. In what few precious moments I had with them,
I wanted to get to know them as best I could.

What you can do. Get up and be present in the workplace. If I were
to do it over again, I would approach it more formally. For instance,
I would have a copy of training schedules handy to see what was
happening at any given time. This would allow me to have the
greatest impact. If a certain event included a large group of people
or had particular training significance, I could visit, assist in training
goals, meet soldiers or boost morale. Make a map of your area, even
as small as it may be and plan your route. Have a list of people in your
organization you want to connect with and check them off as you do
your circulation. When you have exhausted the list, start over.

To better connect with families, use the method I described above to
see what events may have families included in them. In your organization, if you do not already have events bringing families together,
create them. Be cautious of infringing on personal time like weekends and late evenings but find out what might work for your organization. Plan it like you would any important operation and make
a personal connection with families. If you can build in incentives
like child care, food or entertainment, you should do that. Most of all,

make the event worthwhile. Keep it less formal. Do not kill people with briefings and slides. Deliver something short and useful for families then allow for fellowship.

Sensing sessions. I conducted sensing sessions assembling sample populations from my large organization. These sessions would provide me candid feedback from the many sub-cultures or populations in my organization. I could hear from people directly in these sessions in non-attributional dialogue. I kept these sessions no more than one hour in duration and always had my CSM with me as he was the senior enlisted soldier in the brigade. He could be (and often was) a great icebreaker. These sessions were conducted without structure. We would bring a group no larger than 25 into a conference room or lead them under a tree in our unit area, then tell them we wanted to hear from them not ourselves.

In one session, I learned of a paperwork requirement we had placed on units for requesting support for training range operations. It was a redundant requirement which caused more work for our people. Promising to look into it, I did and found it was a self-inflicted requirement which served no purpose. I rescinded it immediately in an official order which I later learned was well received. In other sensing sessions, subordinates expressed displeasure over a rule or situation that was beyond my control. In one session, there was angst over movement dates to an off-post training event which fell on a holiday weekend. The training did not start until after the weekend, so the group was understandably displeased with this infraction on their free time. The answer; we were at the mercy of a larger transportation system that scheduled movement using the most cost-efficient means. This meant weekends and holidays would be stepped on. I wouldn't make the group happy, but they deserved some sort of answer. I told them I didn't like it any more than they did but that I, too, was affected by this rule. My weekend would be taken as well.

I found explaining why things were the way they were and sharing in displeasure instead of trying to justify it worked well.

One of these sensing sessions was conducted with the small population of females in my brigade. I really didn't want to segregate them or make them feel different. They wanted to be treated like any other soldier. I explained I understood their position to them at the opening of the session and it seemed to be well-received. They were fearless addressing me with pointed questions and concerns. We talked briefly about sexual harassment, and I learned that in the barracks, it would most likely occur in the poorly-lit laundry rooms. I had no idea. We addressed it quickly after the session with better lighting and updated evening duty officer routine inspections. I did the same types of sensing sessions with as many sample groups as I could and found it hugely successful. I think perhaps I learned more or got more out of these sessions than the attendees.

What you can do. There is nothing preventing you or your subordinate leaders from conducting sensing sessions. Never pass up an opportunity, planned or unplanned, to gather feedback. The professionals in the True Growth Seminar told me "feedback is a gift" and they could not be more right. You can have these sessions proctored by another leader if you must, but subordinates will want to know their time is well spent and that their concerns will be heard. If you decide to have a proctor, ensure he or she explains how feedback will be sent to you. Your sessions can be as formal or as informal as you desire. Start by identifying the sub-groups in your organization. This does not mean you need to segregate them, but you may get better feedback from a more homogeneous group than one that is too diverse. Furthermore, you might end up mixing people of different authority, and those in the lower rung of your organization may be afraid to speak up. I separated my groups mostly by rank. I would talk to sergeants separately from warrant officers, etc. I found this to be most effective.

Pick the right environment for the session. Be cautious of heavy traffic areas and be sensitive to privacy. Many members will not want what they say to be heard or repeated. Keep them no more than one hour in length. You can offer follow up on-one-on-one meetings as needed. Start the session by notifying everyone that their comments will be non-attributional. It is important to allow members to speak freely. If they have something particularly egregious to mention, you can meet with them separately to discuss it. Of course, you have to be approachable. If you are not, your sensing sessions will be very uncomfortable. Prevent them from turning into whining sessions. If people have complaints, ask them what they suggest as a solution. See if they are willing to be part of the solution instead of just complaining. If the session travels down a rat hole and you are stuck on a single topic, table the topic, gather what you think you need to address it or suggest a deeper study or the forming of a small group to study and address the issue. Try to cover a wide variety of topics in your sensing sessions. Lastly, remember, let them, instead of you, fill up the time talking. Listen!

SENDING PERSONAL NOTES

I took numerous opportunities to send personal notes to soldiers and distant family members like parents and grandparents. Reflecting back, I would have done this more often. When I had witnessed a soldier doing something impressive (which was often) I would ask if it was okay to get an email address for their parents. I'd tell the parent I met their son or daughter that day and would express how well he or she was performing. I would thank them for letting their loved one serve with our team. These notes went over huge. I could imagine the anxiety of a parent or grandparent who worried about their soldier serving in an elite unit like the 101st Airborne Division, a unit with a history of deploying quick and serving in harm's way. I wanted to do what I could to alleviate that fear and thank them for this gift they had given us; this American Soldier, their child or grandchild. I certainly didn't get to everyone but of the ones I did reach; my email was received with enormous gratitude and perhaps some relief that their loved one was healthy and performing well. I did this both at home-station and in combat. It was a small investment, a few lines of email or a text message made a huge impact.

Lucky to have an assistant, I arranged to send anniversary and birthday notes to my leaders across the brigade. Each month, with the help of my S1, my assistant would scan the dates and supply me with typed notes that I could send. I have horrible handwriting so I had them typed but I signed each one often adding a personal phrase of thanks or congratulations. If I saw them around the area, these notes were good reminders for me to recognize them person- ally. I have an old boss who continues to send me emails when it's my birthday. I'm sure he has an electronic calendar or reminder which prompts him to do this but he does take the time to send a note. I continue to be touched by his gestures, especially knowing how busy he is.

What you can do. There is nothing scientific about sending personal notes. If you are as busy as I was, develop a system for it. The best system is to set aside time periodically to identify the dates for key events for your people so you can stay ahead of them. At these times, you could even write the notes in advance and hold them for delivery at the right time. If you do not have an assistant, jot down those who you wish to thank or congratulate and get your cards done at the end of each day or at least each week. Emails and text-messages are okay, but these notes will make a bigger impact than you probably think.

Invest in some nice stationary. Get personal. Use their preferred name or nickname. My assistant had a list of people. Over time, I didn't need it as I had connected enough with those on my list. This simple act and investment of your time may result in an employee going the extra mile for you and the organization. Families will feel the same sense of gratitude.

FAMILY READINESS

As family health and happiness went, so, too did the soldier's. Families made up a population probably three times the size of the brigade. I thought about them constantly. They were worthy of my personal investment. Family readiness meant families that were administratively and emotionally ready for the departure of their soldier into combat. During the Vietnam era and well into the 1980's, Army families were largely ignored by the Army. There were some exceptions but few if any family forums existed where spouses and children could meet unit leaders, see training and deployment calendars, learn more about the skills and functions their soldier performed and receive training and resource links to agencies such as the Red Cross and Army Community Service which would help them through periods of separation, relocation and times of trouble. The old saying went: "If the Army wanted you to have a family they would have issued you one."

Thankfully, the Army took great strides in the 1990s to improve family readiness. No longer was it just a soldier. It was the soldier, his spouse, children, parents, aunts, uncles, etc. Smart. None of us exists without family. Everyone has a significant other or others who have enormous influence on their well-being. Our strong family program would be well-equipped to handle emergencies. If the unit lost a soldier in combat or to an accident in garrison, we would lean on our families to help us grieve and heal. I didn't want a crisis to be the event that caused us to meet each other for the first time.

Regardless of the type of organization, family well-being and inclusion are an important investment. Like Army units, companies do experience emergencies. Many organizations place their employees on the road frequently, sometimes for extended periods. Wouldn't a phone call, an invite to a company event or offer to help go a long way with a family member? Consider if a spouse of one of your employees had car trouble and was not able to rely on his wife as she was traveling. What if the company or a section within the company was prepared to help and the spouse knew this? I know from personal experience that it meant the world to me knowing that support network existed in the organizations in which I served. Consider a well-informed family member, connected to the organization through social and personal networks and what this would mean to your employee. I often found my soldiers were awful at taking information home and sharing it with their spouses. Many of them wanted to leave work at work. I was among them, and sometimes information would never make it to my wife.

Early on in my command tenure, I developed the foundational four pillars to an effective family readiness program. I provide it for you on my website. They are *Structure, Communication Flow, Volunteer Recognition* and *Training and Education. Structure* meant a structure of spouses, partners or fiancés who mirrored our chain of command. Not wanting to use "command" for a family roster, we called it the chain of concern. Structure also meant established and rehearsed notification rosters and procedures for deployment changes, death, injury or other incidents of importance. *Communication Flow* meant a smooth flow of information using phones, social networks like Facebook, emails, etc., so that families were always well informed. A spouse and family may have only been a few miles away from our unit, but sometimes important information struggled to make it to him or her. A formal Communication Flow system was our way to remedy that. We could not pay spouses and families to support unit functions and help us run our FRG. We had to ask for volunteers. To foster volunteerism, we invested time in Volunteer Recognition. This included tracking hours volunteered and hosting awards and functions to recognize the selflessness of our families. Training and Education consisted of instructing spouses on what to do during times of crisis, what steps would be taken to inform and care for families, what agencies were available to help them and what these agencies would provide.

Monthly, my wife Leslie and I would meet with our FRG leaders and their spouses to share information, take feedback and issue guidance. We called this our steering group, and it was a priority meeting for us. My wife Leslie played a huge part. Like me, she had 25 years of experience to bring to the forum and had done all that our subordinate unit leaders had done. We didn't reach every family, and there were some who did not care to be involved. However, I saw enough of them to know we made a difference. Though none of the spouses were paid members, thankfully, they knew the importance of their role. Some had conflicting schedules and demands on them, but all gave what they could. I know it contributed to the health and well-being of the whole brigade and I am forever in their debt.

What you can do. Take the pillars highlighted above and apply them to your organization. Establish a mirror structure with spouses or partners who can call or email from a roster to ensure all are informed. Resource administrative support for this effort either externally or internally by tasking a subordinate agency on your team. Whoever supports the effort, issue some guidance and establish a vision for your version of an FRG such as, "healthy and happy families connected with the organization and prepared for emergencies."

Host organizational functions when it is most convenient for families and carve out a small portion of time to talk about the future of the company and how you see it affecting people. Take time to meet families and attempt to get to know them as best you can. There is nothing wrong with a little training and education. You could educate families on what it is your business, and their loved ones do. You can even bring in experts to deliver non-company related training like water safety during spring months or similar training which may be beneficial to families. These would be great ways to invest in the families of your people. If you have volunteers, keep track of what they do, and if you can, how many hours they give. Recognize and reward them formally. Lastly, imagine a crisis like the death of one of your people and how you might handle it. Spend some time with your leadership and walk through what steps you would take to manage the situation. Visit *www.RobCampbellLeadership.com/Book* for a look at the Family Readiness pillars of my organization.

RESULTS OF INVESTING IN PEOPLE

1st Brigade, 101st Airborne Division led our division (six brigades) in human resource performance throughout the late summer and fall of 2015. We were the top ranking in all the US-based brigades (number one among 34) through the fall of 2015 as I departed command. I took great pride in this accomplishment. It was achieved by leaders like my CSM, my remarkable S1 section and by leaders across the brigade who invested in their people. While I marveled over this feat, there were more indicators I needed to see to determine if our people were invested in. We held the highest retention rate in the 101st Airborne Division for most of my tenure. Soldiers were fulfilled and wanted to stay and serve with us. I witnessed a marked improvement in counseling where leaders were beginning to focus on soldier weaknesses and offer methods for improvement.

Three of my commanders were selected to command (CEO) at the Colonel level, and seven of my majors were selected for command at the Lieutenant Colonel level, a remarkable accomplishment given selection percentages were well below 50 percent. Three of my officers were handpicked to serve directly for the division (one level above brigade) commander. One of my officers was selected to serve as the executive officer for the commander of all US Forces Iraq and another to serve in the White House. Numerous other officers and NCOs were selected above their peers for promotion, command and a variety of other nominative assignments enhancing their careers. For those officers who did not perform as well as their peers, I was able to coach them into assignments that brought them and their family satisfaction. Six officers have transitioned from the Army and are flourishing in business and academia.

Family readiness, which contributed to human resource performance, saw marked improvement. FRG programs which had gone stale in three of my six battalions grew significantly. Family participation increased by approximately 40 percent (measured in several unit functions across the brigade.) Our brigade family readiness program was emulated in subordinate organizations, and I coached leaders from three external organizations on the pillars of our program.

During our combat deployment to Afghanistan, because we had invested in our soldiers, they performed magnificently in a challenging environment conducting themselves with the utmost professionalism. We had zero incidents of misconduct. My forces partnered with Bulgarian, Romanian and African military and civilian security forces protecting a base with over 18 kilometers of perimeter fence. They were lauded for their modern approach to warfare in the latter stages of the Afghan war. When they had to be lethal, they did so with deadly accuracy; when they needed to peacefully engage the Afghan population, they did so with maturity and wisdom and empathy.

I was a three-time combat veteran and a senior officer with over 26 years' experience when I relinquished command. I knew the signs of a combat-ready unit and would call it like I saw it, even if it were my own organization. We lacked some defensive skills and were not as far along in stability operations proficiency as I would have liked, but I could say without reservation, that because we had invested so well in our people I could have deployed the brigade to the world's harshest environment and we would have succeeded. Most importantly, I measured our effectiveness by the personal feedback I received from soldiers and families. I received and still receive personal notes from leaders and soldiers thanking me for taking time to invest in them. This, above all, has meant the most to me. It's proof that through optimistic leadership, my leaders and I made a difference in the lives of others.

Visit *www.RobCampbellLeadership.com/Book* to see my BIO sketch and a method to conduct sensing sessions.

Chapter 6
KNOW YOURSELF

Welcome back to self-awareness. In Chapter 4, I introduced
this topic and shared a few personal stories to help you build
an investing-in-people foundation. In Chapter 5, you learned
more about my self-awareness experience prior to becoming the
commander or CEO of a large organization. Here, I will tell the story
of my own self-awareness exercise, the BIO sketch, to assist with
your own introspection. Though I had done some personality tests
and attended a seminar, the sketch was a great self-awareness exercise for me. It would be shared with over 5,000 people so it needed
to describe me in ways other documents would not. There are many
ways to know yourself. You can reflect informally about what is
important to you, what strengths and weaknesses you have and what
events shaped the person you are. You can take personality tests
as I have suggested or attend a seminar. Or you can combine these
and formally describe yourself in a document such as I have done.
I would recommend the latter.

My overall goal with the BIO sketch was to show my soldiers that
I was a person like them. I was to fill a position of great prestige.
Though I was the highest-ranking man in the unit, I wanted my
soldiers to know me as a person first. I would only accomplish this

by sharing with them how I saw myself. I wanted to be a transparent leader, and I wanted transparency from my subordinate leaders. I felt this would be the best approach to get to know them and for them to know me. In my 25 years before I took command, I had never done a formal document like this. I still use it today.

YOUR PERSONAL BIO SKETCH

To begin, take some time to think about what you want to accomplish with your sketch and what you might want to call it. Recall the environment I described in Chapter 5. That environment, along with the type of organization I was about to command, guided the creation of my sketch. I used "sketch" only to present a different title to make it sound different than a standard biography. Some people are not particularly interested in biographies. I wanted this one to catch everyone's attention. You could call yours "Understanding Ethan Welch," "My Story," or some other effective title. In terms of your purpose you may wish to demonstrate that your values, culture and/or traits align with the organization's. You may want to share hardship, family strife or another life crucible you experienced and how it shaped you as a person and a leader. Below I offer a checklist you could use as a guide to create yours. I'll address the key parts of it in more detail in the paragraphs that follow. Visit *www.RobCampbellLeadership.com/Book* for more about the BIO sketch how to create an effective one.

• •

BIO Sketch

Guidelines

- Be honest! Do not write a sketch for someone you wish to be. Write it about YOU.

- Keep it short. 2 pages max. If you cannot fit all that is outlined below, go with the most important content.

- Sketch is not a place for organizational vision or specifics of what you want to accomplish in the organization. It's about you as a person.

- Only include the most important parts of you. Do not list 12 passions and five life-changing events, just those you feel are most important.

- Avoid turn-offs like political affiliation and deep religious convictions. Okay to state you are a person of faith, etc.

- Avoid including resume-like credentials such as education or certifications unless they had significant impact on you as a person.

- Important to include things you may not be proud of, wish you were better at, failed to do in life, etc. We all have them.

Sketch Content

- Who are you? Name, where did you grow up, siblings, parents?

- What defined you in your youth? What were you passionate about and how did it shape the person you are today?

- What are your passions today and why?

- Traits, characteristics, culture.

- Personality indicators. What best describes your personality?

- What is important to you in the position you hold?

- Share a life crucible and the effect it had on you.

- What are your goals in life (not specific to your duties)?

- How do you want to be remembered after you are gone from the organization? What would you want people to say about you?

- What are your dreams?

- What is it you would love to do before you die?

- What are your fears? What keeps you up at night?

- What sparks your anger?

- What are your strengths and weaknesses and how do you overcome them?

- How do you best operate and receive information? Group think? 70 percent- solution-type person? Details person? Are you more effective in the morning, afternoons?

• •

I'm a person first. Regardless of the type of organization you are in or your specific duties as a leader, your central purpose should be to describe yourself as a person. There may be some stigma attached to the position you hold which is counter to the person you really are. Many Army officers were known to be uptight and completely absorbed in the profession. Subordinates joked that we wore our uniform to bed, read Army tactical manuals while sitting on the toilet and were book-smart geeks unattached to the common folk. CEOs or even some bosses, in general, are thought of as power-hungry, money-grabbing emperors who couldn't care less about the environment, the people below them and anything not related to profit. You won't be able to change the stigma attached to those positions, but you can overcome it by how you conduct yourself. I found that how I described myself was a good first step.

Though I adored the Army and was proud to be absorbed in it, I was not one of those officers who came from a long family history of service or always aspired to wear the uniform and serve forever. I liked that about myself. I had served with a few of these officers in my career, and they seemed a bit narrow-minded and socially inept. I never held automatic grudges against these types of leaders, some were actually very good, and I envied their talents. I just remember many of them and the way they were which did not resonate with me. I always felt there were bigger things than just wearing the uniform. Though I was a career officer, I never really considered myself one. I had other clothes in my closet beside my boots and camouflaged uniform and enjoyed periods where I wouldn't have to shave every day, think about the Army or where I could sleep in late. Early in the sketch, I wrote about why I joined the Army and highlighted the fact that I was never the "chosen one." I wasn't the one selected for early promotions and earmarked for the most prestigious assignments. This displayed for the reader my introspection on how I saw myself more as a person than a soldier. I always felt this and shared it with a few people but never really put it on paper.

How do you see yourself or what did you think you would do when you graduated high school and college? Furthermore, what does it tell you? For me, the message was not to take myself and my job too seriously. Sure, commanding units bound for combat deserved my full attention but so did other things in my life like my family and motorcycles for instance. At the time, I wrote the sketch I did not know how long I would stay in the Army but I knew that I was content at the rank and position I'd achieved and was going to enjoy every day in uniform.

Just a soldier and a regular guy. When I self-reflect, I see a regular guy with faults, worries and doubts like many others. Throughout the BIO sketch, I make mention of them. I was a young man from New England raised by a mother and a father and three sisters who played basketball, practiced my comedy routine in school and worked in a department store. My grades were not good enough to achieve selection for active (full-time) duty status, and I was never selected early for promotion. I just stumbled through my career a regular guy just doing my best. I was selected for and performed well in numerous prestigious positions each of which came as a surprise to me when picked. Whenever I looked in the mirror, I didn't see a super being. I would often gaze in amazement at the rank I was privileged to wear. It helped to reflect that in writing.

Traits. Remember that traits are those qualities you gained in your upbringing. My list of five: Humble, Authentic, Compassionate, Trusting, Critical. There were more, but in my sketch, I wanted these to be reflected as I knew they best described me. These five traits were the end result of a long list of traits that I took and cut down until I arrived at these. I asked myself with each word if it felt right and I weighed how important it was. Under humility, the sketch itself was a symbol of my humility. I took pride in my humility, and I know it came from my dad. He was a very humble and selfless man. In the sketch, I mention my humility being selected for brigade command and I list it as a personal strength. It was a real feeling, and I wanted to share it. I had seen peers and superiors of mine who believed they were destined for or deserved to be in the positions they held. This indicated a huge ego to me, and I didn't want to be seen like that. It wasn't who I was. I was a bit uneasy with the trusting trait. Though I picked it for all the right reasons, I had been burned because of it. In some cases, I put too much trust in a person and was let down. Though I felt that way, I still considered it a strength, but I needed the counsel of those close to me to ensure I was not placing too much trust in someone who was not worthy. These traits were important because they defined me to my core.

Along with positive traits, I wanted to share some negative ones which I worked hard to overcome but which were too embedded in my persona. I determined these, being honest with myself, searching through lists of negative traits. Along with this process, I reflected on criticism I had received in the few counseling sessions I did experience in my career. These traits were ones which I could mitigate by surrounding myself with people who could "protect me from myself," as a mentor once taught me, but ones which I could not shut off, like my humor and sarcasm. I enjoyed being funny and making others laugh but it could and would backfire on me as a leader in a combat arms profession. I would sometimes use my humor as a crutch to cover for a lack of confidence. It was a trait that others would not see coming so I would have to address it myself by being more conscious of it. Being a slow-starter was another negative trait I attributed to my ADD. I knew this deep down after years of reflection and from watching my son struggle with it. It didn't prevent me from leading, but it was something I had to wrestle with my whole life. I was not proud of this but it described me well, and I needed to share it. You, too, have a variety of traits that describe you. Are you quick to anger, a trait you may have picked up from a parent? Do you get emotional? Do you have a strong work ethic? List your traits out and make cuts until you arrive at a true list. Then do something with them. Figure out where you need help to cover your weaknesses or where you might be able to use your strong traits to help others. Share them with your people so they can better serve with you.

Characteristics. I developed numerous characteristics in my growth as a leader in the Army. I narrowed them down to these five: People Person, Good Listener, Enthusiastic, Visionary Thinker,

Inspiring. I wanted to list more characteristics such as innovative, problem-solver and resourceful but I forced myself to pick the ones most important to me. You can see them listed throughout the sketch. I gave this list strict attention and reflected deeply to ensure these were not just desired characteristics but ones I actually possessed and espoused as a leader. I was proud of them and believed they helped me achieve my rank and position. I didn't want to create a "be like me" sketch, but I wanted to show my people which ones I believed were important in hopes they would self-reflect to discover theirs. I was confident I would live out these characteristics in my daily life, and I hoped my humility and my other characteristics would inspire others. Use the same process as you did for traits, create your top five characteristics and then do something with them.

Culture. I wanted to give my BIO sketch readers a sense of my culture. We were all American soldiers of course, but we came from so many different places. My culture defined me, and I wanted to reflect on it and share it with my team. One of my bosses mentioned my New England or Yankee sarcasm and wit in a counseling session. It was used in a negative sense as he tried to tell me how he saw me. The comment was fair, and I believe related to the humor trait I highlighted earlier. When I decided to do some formal self-awareness, this counsel entered my thinking. He was talking about the culture of the Northeast or Yankeedom as Colin Woodard calls it in his book *American Nations: A History of the Eleven Rival Regional Cultures in North America*. Woodard describes the Yankeedom culture in terms of its values of education, intellectual achievement, communal empowerment, and citizen participation in government as a shield against tyranny. I didn't feel there was anything controversial with this culture. Some may not have felt comfortable around it but I wanted to offer it as a way to know me better. Because I was from Massachusetts, I also affectionately labeled myself a "Masshole," which the Urban Dictionary humorously describes as an obnoxious, belligerent, loudmouth who takes pride in his aggressive, illegal driving habits. I've used this term jokingly but with a hint of seriousness to help describe my sarcasm and wit. My traits originate mostly from my upbringing and my Yankee culture. This introspection was both interesting and enjoyable, and I wanted to share it. You can apply the same process to determine your culture. You may want to think about the ethnicity or religion that dominated your upbringing and shaped you as a person. I wouldn't recommend getting into religion in a shared document, but you can certainly describe what is important to you related to the culture you were raised in or which influenced you the most.

Personality. As you saw in my BIO sketch, my interpersonal style (or communicative style) is Expressive. I wanted to include it in my sketch to show my team how I processed information and communicated. This would be important for my staff and subordinate leaders if they wanted to operate more efficiently around me. They would need to know this quickly as we faced many daunting training and administrative challenges that would require subordinate units and staff to communicate with me and obtain decisions. The exercise consisted of picking words that best describe you and transferring the answers to a graph to define your style. It was fun and fostered a true self-assessment. I provide a link to this assessment tool and others on my website.

Along with the interpersonal exercise, I took the Myers-Briggs personality type indicator. This test helped me see how I perceived and judged my environment. The survey took a while, and I wrestled with my answers trying to be as true as I could. I enjoyed reading the description of my ENTP designation and could very much see myself. My wife loved reading it as well, and it even helped her understand me better. One thing among many it highlighted for me was the danger of all my good ideas, innovation, and can-do attitude. It might cause idea overload and extra work for a staff already consumed by the daily running of the brigade. I needed to be conscious of this as well.

Life crucible. Think about what life crucibles you have experienced and how they have shaped who you are today. We all evolve and develop. I was a different leader, a different person as a Colonel than I was as a Captain. My education, experiences and maturity were all contributors to this growth. My father's death, my combat deployments, the growth of my children and my experiences as a father and husband all influenced my life and my leadership. What are yours? Have you gone through a divorce? Did you fail at something very important in your life? What effect did it have on you? The trauma of losing my father and other family members caused me to reflect on and study human behaviors, specifically the ego. This life crucible occurred later in my life as my sons were grown and I achieved the rank of Colonel. It caused me to see people's behavior through a different lens. I would attempt to analyze anger and emotions of myself and others through the prism of the ego and its effect on human beings. It made me more self-aware and able to lead people better. Take time and write down your life crucibles and reflect on what impact they had on you. Pick one or two and include them in your BIO. Talk about them openly. Reflect on how these have shaped you. Take time to understand the crucibles in the lives of your subordinates.

What are your goals in life? How do you want to be remembered after you are gone? What do you want people to say about you after you depart? What keeps you up at night? What reoccurring nightmare do you have and what does it represent? Mine is that I am late for basketball summer camp or I have arrived and have not packed a thing or that I am in school and have not completed my semester's worth of work. It's my eternal fear of being unprepared. Perhaps it's a healthy dream that keeps me on time! What personality traits or characteristics do you possess? Which ones are most important to you? Whatever your story, invest this time in you. You can do it together with your team if you desire. It may actually help if your employees see you letting your guard down to talk about yourself, your strengths, weaknesses, dreams, goals, life crucibles, etc. I didn't share everything in my sketch, but it did reflect some very personal information about me and my life. Share yours with your employees. There is no sense hiding this especially if you truly desire to foster an environment where you invest in your people. Rest assured, your people will definitely see right through you. Not all your employees will willingly want to do this. Some will be hesitant to expose weaknesses as they might believe it may prevent promotion. You have to create the environment where this is accepted. It starts with sharing your own self-awareness with your team.

Visit *www.RobCampbellLeadership.com/Book* for materials on BIO sketch creation and self-awareness.

Chapter 7
KNOW YOUR PEOPLE

Do you want to truly know your people? Easy; move in with them and live with them for six months. Not possible? Okay, then you may have to put into place a process that helps you overcome this. Some believe they already know their people. I challenge this assumption and you should as well. I know my neighbor Danny which is to say, I know his name, where he grew up, what he does for work and that he has a wife and four children. I don't know what his passions are, what personal strife he has experienced in his life and how he might react in a stressful situation. I don't know his dreams, personal and professional goals and if he is fulfilled in his life. Okay, he's my neighbor, isn't that enough? Unfortunately, this is what many leaders consider as knowing their people in the workplace. I call this not knowing or knowing only a collection of facts. Let's imagine Danny is one of our employees. If we were to count on him for an important task, want to give him autonomy or even rely on him to come to our rescue, our current "knowing" of him would be insufficient.

Leading soldiers over the years, I confess I did not know many as well as I should have. It's because I didn't invest enough time in them. I didn't give enough thought to values, characteristics, traits and behaviors. I didn't pause and consider their culture and what it meant. I didn't consider life-shaping events and family demands and conflict that shaped them as people. I didn't dedicate the time to counseling as I should have. Because of this failure, I was surprised a few times when a soldier of mine would behave or react a certain way. As I matured as a leader, father and husband, I gained a deep appreciation for knowing others, and it became my primary quest in every organization I served. It helped me invest in them.

So, what is it to truly know someone? How do you know you have arrived at that point? I've yet to find the formula which tells me this. One of the best measurements or descriptions I have found comes from Corinda Lubin-Katz, a creative writer in New York who says, *"Knowing someone is a cumulation of shared experiences, of stumbling upon mannerisms and quirks. It lends itself to an organic ability to anticipate their reaction to things — to know when and how their anger will thaw, what sparks their passion and what that passion looks like, what constitutes an expression of their love. It's recognizing something as monumental that would appear inconsequential to the untrained — or shall I say unknowing — eye."*

Anticipating the reaction of my people and recognizing the monumental were my goals but it would be hard to accomplish with someone I had just met or only knew for a short while. Time was not on my side. As soldiers, we could deploy on short notice and find ourselves depending on each other with our lives. Getting to truly know someone while under fire would be a risky approach. Even if we were not to deploy, there were some substantial tasks awaiting the brigade and every soldier needed to perform at their best if we were to succeed. Given the social and behavioral health issues in the fall of 2013, I wanted every soldier and leader to recognize the monumental in their buddy so that we could tell if something was wrong and not learn by surprise. My subordinate leaders were all multi-tour combat veterans and had experienced their own trauma. It was my duty to recognize their *monumental* early and address it. We were counting on each other, so we had to truly know each other.

To accomplish my knowing goals, I developed a process I would follow. Nested with my "To Do" list highlighted in Chapter 5, I developed this one specific to knowing our people.

KNOW YOUR PEOPLE

- Know yourself first
- Establish an environment of transparency and knowing
- The BIO Sketch
- The Personal Data Sheet
- Counseling

Of course, the task would begin with me. I would conduct my self-awareness as described and ask my leaders to do the same. I fostered an environment of transparency through my daily communication with staff officers and leaders across the brigade. Along with the BIO sketch that I provided to everyone, I would talk about myself in my initial meetings with subordinate organizations and staff. In these meetings, I focused on what I thought was important, how I processed information and saw my environment and how I desired to know everyone as best I could. I promoted transparency from day one and continued to do so. Using my BIO sketch as my transparency example, I would share info and stories straight off my BIO sketch, both the positives and the negatives. In all my initial counseling sessions, I would focus on the importance of being a transparent leader coaching them to take a similar approach with their subordinates. I also spoke often about knowing and used personal stories to describe the close, transparent relationship I wanted my soldiers to have with their buddies.

The BIO sketch and the sketches I asked my leaders to create for me took me a significant step closer to knowing. I didn't want to prescribe a format or force people to share things they did not want to, but I wanted to get closer to the *monumental*. In some cases, the relationship was too fresh, and I had not established the right level of trust between the subordinate and myself so they didn't share enough. Most used my sketch as a model which was fine. I could sense if someone was not being transparent enough. Naturally, I didn't direct these as a way to pry into someone's personal life. I thought that if I knew what someone might have been struggling with, I might be able to identify it quicker and either help them myself or find help. I used these sketches among other documents and conversations to tailor my leadership approaches to that particular person. Some needed more attention or recognition; some had large egos I knew would be troublesome. Some had mild forms of PTSD. For some, this trauma remained latent below the surface, and they functioned normally. However, this type of trauma could resurface in their behavior and demeanor, and I wanted to know that. I had experienced problems with my own family when my dad fell ill in 2012. Those were trying times for my family, my boss and I, but because he knew me, recognized this. I didn't require his help, but his acknowledgment and concern went a long way with me. By reading the BIO sketches of my leaders and having reoccurring conversations with them, I stood a better chance of knowing if they were having trouble. This knowing would give me a better feel for how they would perform under pressure, lead their organizations and if someday they could handle the responsibilities of my job. Moreover, these sketches would be the icebreaker to a personal and professional relationship I was eager to get started. Connecting with another person in this way was enormously powerful, and I was grateful for their candor and bravery.

Another method I used in my quest for knowing was the personnel data sheet. I've lost count of how many of these I have filled out in a 27-year career transitioning from one unit to another. Many were laborious, rarely used and/or irrelevant. In my counseling sessions throughout my career, I found little use for data sheets. Many were not filled out properly or did not contain the information I really needed. The personnel department often called me anyway when they needed data either because they were too lazy to read it off my sheet, couldn't find it, or had not included the question on the form.

Having said this, the personnel data sheet does have its place in the organization. It should include all the administrative data needed to properly integrate a person and, more importantly, prevent constant administrative questions from personnel managers and leaders. Treat the personnel data sheet as you would the BIO sketch. Make it a priority document. Ensure it only collects relevant information. Attempt to take the labor out of filling out these sheets. Keep them short. The longer and more difficult these sheets are to fill out, the more quality decreases. Formats will vary. Different organizations will require different information. These documents can be a great method to collect information on family, especially spouses and kids. You can include sections that ask what goals the individual has for their children, spouses and themselves. Transform the personnel data sheet from a task to a journey, from work to enjoyment. If this information is in a web-based format, pull it up when you counsel individuals. Have it printed for your interactions with your people and make sure you can access these forms easily. Have them present when you counsel your subordinates to show just how important the document is. Hand these personnel data sheets to your new hires or show them personally where to find them to highlight their impor-tance. By doing this, you set the right tone from the start. Tell them to take the documents home and work on them with friends and family. Keep these sheets handy in hard copy or on a link where you can view them before you head out to visit people. Most importantly prove their worth. Do something with the effort the individual put into filling them out. For instance, help them achieve the goals and dreams they have listed on the sheet. Do all that you can to prevent them from being boring. Ask what passions and interests they have or find another creative way to collect data. Find out where they have lived or traveled in their life. You cannot, nor should you need to know everything. My point is this; dump some energy into this form. Make it fun and worthwhile. I naturally find great interest in other people, where they have been, what their passions are and what they enjoy reading or watching on TV to name a few. Create your own discovery format and make the personnel data sheet personal. Ask your employees what they think.

Touch points and counseling meetings were the most important events in my knowing journey. More on this in Chapter 8, but you really should conduct regular counseling sessions with your subordinates. Some may require more frequent counseling than others. You can do these monthly or quarterly depending on the environment and the individual. I found that quarterly was tough. Three months was a lot of time in-between counseling sessions and I would hate to think of one of my people walking around wondering how he or she was performing. Whatever your frequency, just make sure it is happening. If you actually desire to invest in your people, you will find time. If you do not, you will make excuses about how you are too busy. Lastly, spend time with your people in different settings. If you see Ted daily in the morning update, you will see the same person. If you see Ted during a fun self-awareness exercise or in one-on-one counseling, you will see a different Ted and you will know him even better.

What you can do to "know" your people. Start with my list above and apply it to yourself and your organization. Once you are finished with an extensive self-awareness exercise, have created your own BIO sketch and are ready to foster an environment of transparency, meet with some of your top leaders and HR professional(s) and determine those things you need to know about your people. The elements of my BIO sketch, I submit, are a good baseline. You might need to focus harder on things like culture to see if your people are aligned with your organizational culture. Use questionnaires to determine culture alignment. You will find many surveys that say they are workplace culture-focused but instead focus more on workplace satisfaction. While worthy of your understanding, remember we are trying to know our people. Questions such as rank ordering behaviors like teamwork, innovation and loyalty will tell you more about your people. You can also have them rank order or pick from a set of words to help them understand what they believe is important.

Have them create their own BIO sketches and tell their own story. You will learn a ton. Create a well-thought out personnel data sheet, product or process that helps you know your people better. Place questions on the form that give you a sense of the person. I found a great collection on a site called TinyPulse.com like "Who inspires you?" Or, "What's the craziest thing you've ever done?" Bring in self-awareness or development seminars that assemble your people to share their stories for the betterment of themselves and the team. You can also contact a leadership consulting organization and describe your knowing objective and see if they can help. Quiz your leaders often about their people. Test their knowledge to see if it is at the depth you would desire. Lastly, get a productive coun-seling program started. Ensure it is a program promoting transpar-ency and requires the counselor and counselee to meet in person periodically. Join me in the next chapter, and I will outline how best to conduct counseling.

Chapter 8
COUNSELING AND DEVELOPING PEOPLE

In this chapter, we will delve deeper into two of the most important activities associated with investing in people: counseling and development. So far in this book, you have been introduced to both through stories and from my own experience. Here, I will walk you through both in greater detail highlighting some pitfalls and offering methods to overcome them. I placed special emphasis on these two activities as I knew they were central to our success or failure. This same emphasis is needed in any growing organization.

COUNSELING

I use counseling not in a psychological sense as you would visit a counselor for mental health reasons, rather in a performance sense like a monthly or quarterly meeting with a supervisor to review job performance, determine personal and professional strengths and weaknesses and work on growth. Some leaders are very comfortable and effective at counseling a subordinate. Many struggle greatly with this task and it winds up at the bottom of the "to do" list. Some leaders are uncomfortable looking another in the eye to offer criticism or tell them they have failed or are failing. Some are uncomfortable describing the flaws of another in a one-on-one session, so they keep it to themselves. Those being counseled may be uncomfortable sharing personal information or exposing weaknesses. Their ego may cause them to be defensive. They may not take criticism lightly. They may not want to hear the truth or how others view them. They may fear being fired (which should send alarm signals to leaders.) Because of this, the task gets dropped. The counselor does not place priority on this event; the counselee does not push the boss to conduct the counseling.

Throughout my lengthy career, I can count on one hand the number of effective counseling sessions I have experienced. Of the ones I have experienced, many of them were dry and impersonal. My boss treated the session as a task that needed completion, not a journey we could take together or an opportunity for him to pass on wisdom and experience or let me discover why I was not performing at my peak. In some of them, my supervisor did all the talking. I never had a chance to speak other than being asked: "Do you have any questions?" Some of my superiors were not interested in what I had to say. In these cases, I would ask the question he failed to ask. "What do you believe are my weaknesses?" or "How do I measure up against my peers?" In the good sessions, I was asked hard questions like "Tell me what your weaknesses are?" Or, "How do you think your peers would describe you?"

Amidst all of this, people still desire feedback and counseling from their leaders. A Gallup study indicated that over 60 percent of global employees report receiving too little feedback and a quarter of them report that they received no feedback at all from their supervisors–a major factor in their workplace dissatisfaction. Everyone needs counseling, even the most senior leader. I was a seasoned combat veteran and 25-year leader of soldiers when I took command of a brigade. However, I had never been a brigade commander before. Leadership at this level took on a different form. Like all officers, I was still growing as a leader and needed a good dose of counseling from my superior. I needed to hear how he viewed my performance and I needed to tell him how I saw myself. I needed his seasoned advice and counsel on how to better lead my organization. These were conversations I was willing and eager to have, and I knew my subordinates were as well.

As I stated, investing in people activities such as counseling took up at least one-third of my calendar, perhaps even more as I would turn standard meetings and forums into investment opportunities. I was the leader at the center of this effort, so I had to be its main practitioner. I couldn't hand this task off to another person or do it by email. I had doubters try to convince me it could not be done. Many claimed that I would be consumed by the "shiny object" or crisis of the day or that I would be too busy running a large organization. There certainly were days which swallowed me but this was a priority, and I had a team of fantastic soldiers to help me run the brigade. I had served long enough and screwed this up a few times, so I knew I was right. I chose to approach counseling as I would a combat patrol, with detailed preparation and execution.

I found flaws in my own organization when I inspected soldier counseling. Some were very good, but many lacked a personal focus, offered vanilla feedback and failed to offer tools and objectives for improvement. These had little relevance to individual growth. I found too many that focused more on unit activities instead of the individual. The counselor would describe what the unit had done over the last 30 to 90 days as a way to review past events and prepare individuals for future ones. These "unit activities" focused counseling sessions were of little value. The counselee could have read unit activities on a calendar. In other counseling packets, I would find comments like "Your motivation and leadership are good." Or, "You need to keep improving or strive to be better." Or, "You need to improve your marksmanship or 2-mile run time." These comments were marginally helpful to an individual and showed a lack of effort or a leader just trying to check off a task instead of making a real difference in someone. While skill improvement such as marksmanship was important and deserved leader attention, I was looking for my leaders to address characteristic development and highlight obstacles individuals were facing to achieve growth like lack of patience or too many emotional displays or a big ego. I wanted these sessions to be enormously valuable to the counselee. I wanted leaders to have really accomplished something by the time the session ended. I wanted them to challenge, inspire, discover and grow each person.

So, how do you do this? In the paragraphs ahead, I will outline my approach to counseling. There are several creative ways to format the counseling form and conduct the session to achieve good effects. Remember you must be counseling a subordinate against an agreed-upon set of values, vision culture, etc. As I mentioned in Chapter 4, if you do not have your foundation built, your counseling program will be at risk of failure. For a sample of the form I used, visit my website. Think about what end state you have in mind for the counseling session. In other words, when the counselee departs the session what will you want to have accomplished? You may want the counselee to leave with a fresh assessment of what obstacles stand in the way of them achieving efficiency or advancement in the organization. Or it could be to discover a counselee's true passions. Whatever you decide, document it and set aside some time to do it. Too many people, not enough time and constant disruptions will always be reasons to not counsel. Use my leadership principles to overcome this challenge. Do everything you can to overcome these distractions. Checklist time again! Below is a checklist for counseling preparation. After preparation, I will offer a method to conduct the counseling then finish with developing people.

PREPARE FOR THE COUNSELING SESSION

- Preparation
- Establish the Environment
- Allocate Sufficient Time
- Gather Supporting Documents

Preparation. Counseling is too important to be unprepared. This one-on-one meeting, if done right, could have a behavior-changing impact on an individual. It should not be treated as a casual get together like a social date for a cup of coffee. Also, because counseling happens so infrequently, every three months, for instance, preparation is vital. Consider the impact you would like to have on the counselee and compare it to the impact you would want to have on a group of people to whom you were trying to sell an idea or product. You would invest a lot of time and preparation into an event like that.

In most cases, the counselee will arrive nervous, anxious and having thought a lot about what they will say or how they will address your questions and potential criticism. You should arrive as well-prepared as the counselee. I spent my preparation reviewing the BIO sketch, looking over previous counseling, talking briefly to immediate supervisors, finalizing my notes, printing off any professional articles I wanted to use to reinforce my points and establishing the environment. I also had a look at their data sheet to see if there were any significant personal or professional events coming up for them. There were times when my schedule did not afford me the preparation time I would have liked. In those instances, I would usually walk out of my office, acknowledge the individual and ask for a few moments. I would use this time, which cut into the actual counseling session to do some hasty preparation. At a minimum, I would read over the BIO sketch. The preparation part was important enough that I used part of the allocated hour to do it. I was lucky to have a staff. They could assemble all the required documents for me which saved time and allowed me to get personal quickly and effectively.

Establish the environment. I always strove to set the perfect environment for counseling sessions, but I would not let the inability to establish that environment stop me from conducting them. If I had to, I would find a quiet corner in a room and huddle with the counselee. To maximize the effect, I would conduct these sessions in my office. There, I could use my dry erase board if I needed to illustrate a point. I could also obtain a professional article or access my computer files as needed. Sometimes, I did go to the location of the counselee. That too was helpful, so I could get a feel for their environment. Was their office in shambles? Was it overly neat? The answer to these questions helped describe the person. Regardless of the location, my cell phone was off and away from me, my computer screen was shut off, the conference table in my office was cleared of everything except the documents pertaining to the counselee and my dry erase board was sterilized. My staff would accept my calls and interrupt only if necessary.

Allocating sufficient time. I would schedule counseling for one hour. Depending on what I had next on my calendar, I would let the session extend beyond one hour if needed. My intent was to counsel to standard (achieving the objectives) and not to time (one hour then stop). I didn't want to be like the unconcerned psychiatrist in the movies, "Time's up!" If for some reason, I had a follow-on appointment,

I would offer a follow-up with the individual if needed. Along with sufficient time to conduct the session, I would avoid bad times like very early morning or late afternoon, especially Fridays. Mornings were my preference, and I avoided the Friday afternoon periods, but I would not stop from scheduling counseling during these times. It had to be done so I would do it whenever I could.

Gather supporting documents. For supporting documents, my counseling packets contained a personnel data sheet, an officer's career and records summary, previous efficiency reports (if the officer was willing to share, because legally I could not direct this), the BIO sketch and a career timeline. The career timeline included promotion and command selection board dates for that specific officer so that we could explore potential career opportunities. I also had ready the new counseling form that contained my thoughts and review of their performance aligned with our unit's vision and values. I could add documents as needed based on my counseling objectives. For instance, I could bring in performance statistics from that person's unit if I needed to make a point. This, I believed was enough to help me properly counsel a subordinate. I would not refer to all these documents, but they were there if I needed them.

CONDUCT THE COUNSELING SESSION

- Outline the counseling agenda
- Let them start the conversation
- Get to weaknesses or areas where improvement is needed
- Describe how you see them and their performance
- Cover administrative as needed (qualification scores, technical performance data)
- Review the session and goals for the future (career timeline)

- Thank them for their time and candor and offer to help them anytime they need it

Preparation complete, I was ready. I would personally escort the counselee into my office, tell them where to sit, then sit near them in a relaxed posture to help them relax. I would never counsel from behind my desk (talk about impersonal.) I wouldn't rush for papers or dive right into the session. I wanted to focus on them, get a feel for their demeanor and try to help them relax. I was eager to have them talk instead of me. Once the environment was set, and I had done what I could to make them feel relaxed, I would start. In the initial counseling sessions, I would outline the agenda, so they knew what to expect.

COUNSELING AGENDA

- Your Personal Update
- Strengths and Weaknesses
- My Assessment of You
- Career Timeline Review
- How Can I Help?

In subsequent sessions, I skipped this part and got personal as fast as I could. I would always ask "So, how's it going?" This was my way of opening the door for them to start the conversation and share their challenges. Many would talk about their unit's accomplishments deflecting the spotlight away from themselves. While I appreciated their selflessness and was genuinely interested in their unit's activities, these sessions were personal. What I wanted to hear was how *they* were doing, good and bad. If I accomplished nothing else in a counseling session "So, how's it going" would be the most important question and discussion. Sometimes I had to coach them into the answer I was looking for. I would counter with: "No, *you* personally, how are *you* doing? What are *you* struggling with?" I could always find out how their unit was doing and likely already knew. Hearing about the greatness in their lives was good and important, but we would not end up talking about that much. I wanted to get to the stuff that needed repair.

From this point, I would move into asking them to describe their weaknesses. This question could cause another pause or deflection from the counselee. They might grow uncomfortable during this part of the session. I had a few officers who had trouble coming up with an answer. This might indicate that their ego was too big or they had not done any self-reflection. Perhaps they were terrified to expose a weakness. It was very important to me that they felt comfortable sharing their weaknesses. Sometimes, I would wait for an answer in the awkward silence. Some would describe technical or physical weaknesses such as having weak written communication skills or being a slower runner. This is not what I was looking for. To help with this misunderstanding or deflection, I would offer up my own weaknesses. I would tell them how I tend to miss small details in meetings and in conversations and that I had too much patience at times. Letting my guard down and opening up a bit usually made for a very open and authentic discussion. I could help them with poor writing skills or help them improve their level of physical fitness, but we didn't need a focused one-hour session to work on things like that. This approach usually opened the door and got the conversation going. Once the counselee opened up, I could start to help them through their weaknesses personally or consider other methods to help them. Solutions did not come quick and easy, but in many cases, I had experienced a similar situation and had overcome it.

In the cases where I didn't possess the experience or knowledge to address a counselee's weakness(s), I worked with them to discover who could help or how they might help themselves. The sweet spot was identifying the weaknesses. Regardless of whether I could help or not, it was very beneficial for the counselee to talk about it. Once done, I could work with the counselee to address the weakness or find ways to mitigate its effects. The objective was to get to something real. Moreover, I wanted *them* to identify the problem(s) and solution(s). I could offer a dozen solutions, but the best ones would be the ones self-discovered. This was the heart of the counseling session, and if all I accomplished was this, I had done my job. If a serious behavioral issue was discovered, the counseling session would obviously take a significant turn. It could be a situation requiring immediate attention. Thankfully, I was prepared for that with professionals to call upon.

Following our discussion on personal weaknesses and how to address them, I would then have a chance to describe how I viewed them and their performance. If I was doing my job, my description would match how the individual viewed themselves. My approach here was centered on our organizational vision (how we saw ourselves) and our values. Alignment with our vision and values was essential to me. I knew if they were aligned and believed what I did I could count on them and their unit. I assessed the character, values and traits like humility, patience, optimism and team-play that I believed were commensurate with our profession and required for their advancement in rank and position. I would outline these along with other focus areas like combat readiness and their investment in people then walk them through each one. I covered them all, the positive and the negatives. I spent more time on the negatives and charged them with improving areas they were weak in or where I saw misalignment in their organization. I owed them some honest personal feedback on their performance. If they or their unit were under-performing in areas like counseling or combat preparation, it was here I could address it and direct them to fix what was wrong. It was very important to me that they leave our session knowing how I assessed them and how I assessed their potential measured against Army expectations and their peers in the organization.

Lastly, I would review their professional career timeline to examine what they needed to do to advance given their potential. Having traveled the path before them, I was able to offer advice on what steps to take. Here I could give them a dose of reality as well. Not all my officers were going to be generals. From their previous efficiency reports and my assessment of them, I could tell them if I thought they were competitive for advancement. It was here I could determine the officer's career desires and my role in helping them. Some needed a boost either in their efficiency report or with another career-enhancing assignment to make them competitive for advancement. In the Army, career projection needed to occur one-year ahead of the next assignment. I wanted to get ahead of this process to keep my officers competitive and serve them and the Army properly by placing them in the right job. Few ever did this for me in my career. I was largely left alone to figure this out for myself or to work it out with a personnel manager who didn't know me personally.

I would close the session reviewing what we had talked about, what goals were established and how I was prepared to help. My objective was to have the counselee depart the session with greater self-awareness and authenticity, with established goals and tools to overcome their weaknesses. I wanted them to know I cared and was interested in their growth and fulfillment regardless of the path it would take them on. I would use the notes from this counseling session as a review of future ones. We could not solve all their problems and address all their weaknesses in one hour, but we sure could cross very important territory. It was personal, not personnel.

DEVELOPMENT

Counseling, if done properly, is absolutely a form of development, however; counseling without development is not enough to properly invest in people. As I highlighted in Chapter 3, people want growth. While there are some who are content with the position they hold, I've found them to be the exception. Most want to advance personally and professionally. My goal in command was to ensure we both had a sound organizational and individual development program. I wanted to develop people at every opportunity, formal and informal and I wanted to broaden the minds of my officers. A typical Army officer's career path was dotted with leader development courses, so my officers and I were used to continuous learning and growing. While development had institutional emphasis across the Army, I did serve in units that under-emphasized this, approached it from a very narrow perspective or failed to effectively develop individuals altogether.

In almost every area where my brigade performed poorly, I could trace its cause to a gap in our development program. For example, we came in second in a division-wide competition one summer. I wanted to win first place as it was a great opportunity to showcase the brigade in front of our entire division and foster some pride in our soldiers. The competition was ours to lose. We had dominated all but one event. This event consisted of a series of physical and combat-related drills, and it was given extra weight in terms of points more than any other. We lost it and the competition because we did not place emphasis on fielding teams to win this event. The loss bothered me not only for the missed opportunity but because it highlighted a gap in our leader development which I know would have prevented this. The teaching point was this: Think like the boss or the commander and not like an administrative assistant or staff officer. The goal of the staff officer appointed to direct and coordinate our preparation was to ensure we had the required number of teams (task to be completed.) My goal was to win the competition (intent of the boss.) This could have been achieved easily by soliciting my help to direct units to provide their very best teams for the event we lost. We would have won. I should have directed him to brief me on how we could achieve victory thus meeting my intent. He should have thought about his task through my lens and not just task completion. This scenario would have made a great leader development session where we could have used vignettes like this to teach our officers to think beyond task completion or measure of performance to task intent or measure of effect.

While I remain proud of our development efforts in my organization, if I were to start again I would add a few things. I would have included self-development as one of our development topics in our program and would have added it as a formal agenda item for counseling. I would have published and updated a professional reading list symbolizing our values and vision. I would have worked harder to carve out more space for leader development events. I would have invited more experts such as academics, other governmental agency professionals and historians to better prepare my team for the environments where we would serve.

ORGANIZATIONAL DEVELOPMENT

In 2014, the Army re-released the Army Training and Leader Development (ATLD) official guidance. ATLD provides a useful definition for developing leaders. *"Leader development is the deliberate, continuous, sequential, and progressive process — founded in Army values — that grows Soldiers and Army Civilians into competent and confident leaders capable of decisive action. Leader development is achieved through the life-long synthesis of the knowledge, skills and experiences gained through the training and education opportunities in the institutional, operational and self-development domains."*

Bravo! Replace *Soldiers* and *Army Civilians* with *X Company Employees* or *Team Members* or *People*, simplify it a bit (the Army loves lofty, heavily-worded definitions) and you have a useful definition for your organization. Try this one out: *Developing people in Company X is the deliberate and continuous process, grounded in our company's values and culture designed to produce the future leaders of our industry. We will embrace every opportunity, formal and informal, through counseling, education and self-development to invest in our people.*

The Army did commendable work developing selfless leaders of character who could lead people under the most stressful conditions. Often, in Army courses throughout our careers, we would study ethics, decision making, history and hone our leadership skills to name a few. I was fortunate to have that institutional backing as officers and NCOs arrived in my organization. I had a good development definition (ATLD) as a start point. I just needed to tailor development to my organization. Thinking formally about this, I developed a list of questions I would use as my measuring stick in command.

- "Is my development program deliberate and continuous?"
- "Was it grounded in our values and capable of producing the next generation of Army leaders?"
- "Was it too narrow in focus?"
- "Were my officers self-developing?"
- "Were my leaders developing their people?"

The answer to these questions was very important to me, and I used them to form my assessment when I took briefings from units and spoke to leaders. As I described in Chapter 5, along with investing in our people, we needed to return to offense, stability and defensive core proficiency to establish a good combat readiness foundation. Just as important, we needed to develop leaders with broad minds able to assess complex environments and tailor their methods and organizational structure to operate in them. For instance, we knew that the key to success in a future combat zone might have nothing to do with finding and finishing the enemy. It may actually require socio-economic solutions not typically taught in Army learning institutions. We needed utility infielders, not one-trick ponies. We summarized this in our shared vision and along with a solid set of Army Values, we established our program. Having identified gaps in combat proficiency during my day one session with commanders, we had a good start point in understanding the problem before we developed a program. I designated three of my subordinate organizations as centers of excellence (COE) in offense, stability and defense in that order of priority. They would do the research and develop the periods of instruction for leaders across the brigade. Along with this, I solicited the help from a few colleagues experienced in the socioeconomic domain to come educate my leaders. We established a baseline of topics at the brigade level then gave subordinate units autonomy to fill in the rest of the development menu based on their environment, specific function, our vision and the Army Values.

This formal organizational development program would not be enough. It had to be continuous, so I would look for opportunities everywhere, every day. One area where I found opportunities was in our standard reoccurring meetings. When we failed to meet a directive or fell below established standards, I would conduct a hasty development session to arm my leaders with concepts, philosophies and methods designed to grow them. This would accomplish a lot. It would soften the blow of failure and show my people that rather than dwell on the letdown I was willing to learn and develop with them. Their failures were my failures and I would take corrective action where needed but more importantly, I wanted to develop my team during these challenging periods.

In one instance, we had failed to meet a deadline set by our higher headquarters on a property accountability issue. In our panic to correct the failure, we caused a disruption to some important leader training events we had previously scheduled. Examining the problem and its causes, I quickly discovered we would only be a few days late and had a good reason for it. I know our headquarters would have understood and accepted the delay. We just hadn't communicated that to them. I gathered the leaders involved and identified the failure as a lack of communication and foresight more than a missed suspense. I then spoke about the importance of organizational communication and effective ways to manage deadlines while preventing turbulence. I recalled stories from my past where I had failed at the same thing to show that I, too, failed and learned just as they did. This type of scenario played out several times in my tenure as commander. Often, it was the spur-of-the-moment development opportunities that contributed to our growth the most.

What you can do. As the leader of an organization, without an institutional development program to fall back on, develop one to suit your team. Start, as everything should with the organization's vision, values and culture. From that start point, work with a small group of leaders to determine existing developmental gaps and objectives for education and training. Create an ATLD-like definition to describe the program then establish COEs or find people possessing the requisite experience and/or skills inside your organization to form and conduct education and training. I would also strongly consider outside professional agencies that could help. You need utility infielders so consider development that would foster this.

For instance, your finance department should understand how the product development department functions and vice versa, the goal being broader awareness and knowledge. Additionally, train your organization on how to assess external environments and their effect on the organization to make you more competitive and foster growth. For instance, think about a college professor or similar professional who you could pay to educate your team on government regulation, environmental policy or current innovation in your industry. Make use of videos coupled with discussion sessions for development. Pick a controversial topic and have two groups debate a theory or position.

INDIVIDUAL DEVELOPMENT

As you have seen in the previous chapters, numerous people are suffering from job dissatisfaction for a variety of reasons, not the least of which is lack of development. So why is it many organizations do little to develop their people? Some play the "too busy" card; some do not see the tangible benefits to developing their people or believe it will happen on its own over time. Some leaders are frightened by it. They believe this investment might lead to their own replacement or that their people may depart and join another organization. Peter Baeklund, a performance specialist, offers this scenario to counter that theory, CFO asks CEO: "What happens if we spend money training our people, and then they leave?" CEO: "What happens if we don't, and they stay?" Going a step further, Richard Branson the founder of The Virgin Group states, "Train people well enough so they can leave, treat them well enough, so they don't want to." The tangible effects of developing people cannot be overstated. People joining the workforce are seeking just that. In a survey conducted by Jumpstart HR, a consulting company, overwhelmingly, the employed and unemployed responded that they are hoping to land their next job with a company where they can increase their skill set. Development beat out compensation and benefits, company culture, and company brand as the most important factor in determining whether candidates would submit an application.

I knew walking into command we would establish a sound development program at the organizational level. I had the Army's institutional backing and a strong team of leaders who would create an innovative, effective program. I was eager to get an individual development program started. It would, of course, be tailored to the individual rather than a generic approach for the benefit of all. Discovery of individual development needs would be the best part, and I was eager to get started. The plan was pretty simple. Get personal. Counsel (as described in this book) and get to know your people and their developmental needs. The hard part might be how to actually conduct the development, but I saw this as a leadership challenge, one which I was ready to take on.

As I expected, I found myriad developmental opportunities through my counseling of my leaders. Some officers had been in tactical units far too long and needed a developmental job away from the "muddy boots" Army to broaden their mind such as time with other services like the Air Force or Navy or on a college campus in an advanced civil schooling program. For others, I could simply prescribe a book, video or professional article to challenge and expand their thinking. Where their needs exceeded my abilities, I would connect them with someone who could help. For instance, a colleague of mine had spent several years working in and with the US Government Interagency. One of my officers desired a future there, so I connected the two of them. If it was a writing deficiency, I could assign them a professional writing assignment and find an officer with an English degree and team them up. Some, quite frankly, needed to separate from the Army and take off on another developmental journey, one the Army could not provide. In those cases, I personally assisted in their transition from the Army into another developmental career.

Some development was not specific to occupational skills, but I believed it to be development just the same. I had one officer learning a second language. Another was taking courses in real estate. Some had hobbies needing support. We had several motorcycle riders in the brigade, and I allowed them to conduct riding events during the week. While it may not have made them better mechanics, intelligence analysts or riflemen, it did promote their growth and health and in many cases, broadened their minds. I saw this as a benefit to the organization, so I wanted to assist.

Along with what I would do for them, I wanted to know what my people were developing themselves. In my career, I pursued a master's degree, took additional courses in the Army schools I attended such as a class designed to produce a web-based professional forum for Army majors and a course on the morality of war. I also did some professional reading and increased my study of history. I knew I needed this to keep pace with a rapidly changing and competitive Army and I wanted to know what my officers were doing in this area. The Army provided countless opportunities for self-development, and I wanted my people to take advantage of it.

What you can do. Leverage the organizational development approach I outline above then get personal. Connect with all your people to determine what development they require. You can even place that question on a personnel data sheet or include it in your counseling program. You can ask your people to identify their top professional, and personal development requirements. Most importantly, do something about it. Consider these examples to inform your own approach. Jayson is a financial officer who displays leadership qualities and potential for advancement. Along with

Jayson's job-focused development courses, the company could pay for or assist with college courses or leadership training or allow him to shadow an organizational leader. Christine lists one of her personal development goals as learning a second language. Perhaps the company could fund her language training or allow her to take time off to pursue this goal. The company might even be able to leverage that new skill in the organization. Under this individual development approach, both these employees will likely come to work with a greater sense of duty and motivation to help the organization succeed.

Be ready to develop at every opportunity. Be prepared to pause and assemble employees to turn good and bad situations into developmental opportunities. Along with development which grows employees in their core functions, bring in outsiders who can help foster creativity in learning and development. Poll your people to see what topics they might be interested in or what personal goals they have which may turn into developmental opportunities. There is nothing like a mind that has been exercised. That mind, having experienced something different than it does day in and day out, will serve the organization and the individual far better.

Visit *www.RobCampbellLeadership.com/Book* for additional materials on counseling.

Chapter 9
MEASURING EFFECTIVENESS

Any activity designed to invest in people and bring the "personal" into "personnel" must be measured no matter how big or small. Even if it's just you, the boss, wanting to implement something for your eight employees, measure it. I've been in too many organizations that prided themselves on developing a great program or plan but failed to put measurements in place that would tell them whether their plan was succeeding. For those organizations that did measure, many used bad measurement processes giving them useless or false indicators. The most frequent problem I have encountered is confusion between measuring effects or performance. Department of Defense Joint Publication 3-0 defines the difference. Measures of effectiveness (MOE) should answer the question, "Are we creating the effect(s) or conditions in the environment that we desire?" Measures of Performance (MOP) measure if a task was completed.

If one of my units went to a rifle range and achieved 100-percent qualification of all its assigned riflemen, I would view this as a MOP. While an important data point, what I would want to know is the MOE: *How many qualified expert and how well did they fire under stress?* 100-percent qualification is of course, very important but the effect I want is riflemen who can employ their weapon with deadly accuracy even under duress. Knowing the difference between MOP and MOE is vital for the success of your investing-in-people program. You should measure both, but I would submit MOEs are most important. To further illustrate, if an employee were counseled four times over the last year that is a MOP (task completed). While it is important to know counseling is happening, if the counseling did not address weaknesses or obstacles to growth or if it wasn't done in person, it failed to deliver the effects of truly investing in a person.

So, why is it we are so attracted to MOPs over MOEs or that MOE is overlooked? There are two main reasons. First, we are too accustomed to measuring performance and second, measuring effects is time-consuming and difficult.

Too accustomed to measure performance. Think about the reports you submit in your organization. Most of them report performance measures such as: "Annual ethics training was completed." "The project was funded." Or, "Every member qualified with their weapon." Instead of effects: "People have greater ethical awareness and are conducting themselves ethically." "The project is producing the effects we developed it for." And "every member can shoot accurately even under stress." In Iraq and Afghanistan, the Army fell into the MOP trap. Units would measure the number of enemy killed or captured or number of artillery rounds fired (MOP) and believe they were achieving success if numbers were high. For instance, Unit A which killed more enemy during its tour than Unit B might seem to have performed better. However, if Unit A left behind an area more unstable than the one they found, they accomplished very little toward achieving war's end: the ultimate goal. This performance data might actually indicate that Unit B was more effective. Unit A picked a fight each day. Unit B conducted activities to stabilize its area thus causing a decrease in violence resulting in less enemy killed, and fewer artillery rounds fired.

Measuring effects is time consuming and difficult. It is true that MOEs are harder to measure. But you have to do it to be effective. I could look at a spreadsheet or a slide and see quickly if efficiency reports were being completed before their deadline. The effect these efficiency reports had on the betterment of my people and the ability of my leaders to write and deliver an effective efficiency report would be harder to determine and to display graphically. Furthermore, it would take time to collect this information. Addressing the challenge of sexual assault and harassment in my organization, my higher headquarters, focused on MOPs, wanted to know if I had unit advocates designated, trained and certified and if I had conducted annual mandatory sexual assault and harassment training. I could easily tell them that. What I wanted to know was if the trainer and training were effective at educating my people on the signs and prevention of harassment and assault and if we had chosen advocates who could help decrease incidents in our organization and who soldiers trusted. Most importantly, the effect I wanted to measure was the confidence my soldiers had that they would not be harassed or assaulted and that if it happened, they felt comfortable reporting it and confident their leaders would take action. Through surveys, sensing sessions and from conversing with soldiers and leaders, we would come closer to answering effectiveness indicators. We would discover levels of trust and learn where assault and harassment were likely to happen and we were able to pick passionate, respected advocates, however, we would never have perfect clarity as we might in viewing a MOP. My leaders, advocates and I would have to work constantly to answer our MOEs.

How you can do it. There are several ways you can measure if your investing-in-people program is succeeding. I've summarized them for you below. The list is not all-inclusive as I am sure there are other innovative ways to measure effectiveness. Take this list, assemble a team and develop MOEs for your efforts.

- Organizational and customer service surveys
- Productivity and other performance indicators
- Employee turnover rate
- Sensing sessions
- Visiting and talking with your people

Surveys, I have found are one of the best ways to determine if you are achieving effects. However, they require thoughtful creation and implementation, or they will be of little use. Avoid the typical survey pitfalls. Do not make them too long. Ten questions are as long as you want them to be, but five is better. Be deliberate with the questions. Give each one detailed analysis to determine what you want it to tell you and beta test your surveys to see if they are user-friendly. Surveys that require written responses are very helpful but are risky in terms of getting respondents to commit time and effort answering them. Additionally, be cautious of when you decide to administer surveys. Think about what times are best for respondents. Friday afternoons, at the end of the work day for your team members are poor times, or for customer service people, the point of sale, is usually a bad option. Provide an incentive. Let employees depart early for the day once complete. Keep them anonymous. This can be hard to do in small organizations, but you should attempt to keep from knowing the survey's author.

You can and should measure customer satisfaction. As a customer, I've seen numerous surveys focused on how I was treated by an employee or how helpful and courteous I found the employees. The answers on customer service surveys can tell you a lot about the demeanor of your people which can lead to determining employee fulfillment, alignment with vision, etc. They might also be indicators that supervisors are not engaged with their people and aware of their daily behavior. You can tailor these customer service surveys toward specific effectiveness measures. For instance, if problem-solving is a characteristic you want your employees to espouse, ask specific questions on a survey about whether employees helped customers solve their problems. Your question can have a numeric value (1= most satisfied, 5= least satisfied) to give you a quick assessment. Questions can be more specific to determine the eagerness an employee displayed in problem-solving or the efficiency in which they problem solved.

Organizational surveys can be very informative for leaders who are trying to measure their people investment. I assembled a team of smart, mature officers in my brigade to help create the surveys I wanted to conduct. One was a climate survey where I asked questions about how much the unit leadership listened to its people and whether subordinates thought the leadership team at the top of the unit was synchronized in its guidance and direction for the unit. Another dealt with the level of trust soldiers had in their leaders to help them with a sexual harassment or assault claim. Get creative. In a survey on the quality of counseling, for instance, ask specific questions such as "Did your supervisor ask you to share your personal weaknesses in your last counseling session?" Do you feel the leaders of this organization are helping you identify and achieve your goals?" You can ask open questions like "Do you feel stressed at work?" You will want supporting narrative. You could follow the question with "If you answered yes, please list the top three things which cause you work stress." Or, "Please explain."

Indicators like productivity, employee turnover and operational efficiency can contribute to measuring effects although you have to be able to link the data to specific MOEs. For instance, increased sales could simply mean market conditions have changed. However, if you can trace sales increases to a change in employee assimilation to the company's culture because of focused development training you have conducted, then you know you are achieving effects. This is tricky, but you can create survey questions that will help you determine the effects loyal employees have on sales. Better yet, you can conduct sensing sessions and have open dialogue to find out if there is a relation. I have found that the more difficult the path is to measure effects, the easier you have to make the process. A sensing session allows for two-way dialogue. Refer to Chapter 5 for my approach to sensing sessions. The only caution I offer is to balance the time the group gets to talk against the questions you have to help you measure effects

Here is another way to measure effectiveness. Get up and walk around. As I highlighted in Chapter 5, walking around my unit area talking to people was invaluable. If you have certain MOEs in mind, carry along a handful of questions and head to areas where you know there will be people who can give you the feedback you need. I used to start discussions where I would offer a combat scenario and ask what their reaction would be. This was a great way to determine if our modern warfare vision was understood and embraced. You can gain a great deal, perhaps more than what any survey can tell you by walking around and talking to people.

CONCLUSION

Reflecting back on my life to date it amazes me how much our environment has changed. I lived in the same town until I was 23. My dad sold commercial insurance for more than 40 years with the same company. During his tenure as a salesman, the economy ebbed and flowed. Even through all of this, there was a sense of stability. The company was not going to let my father go overnight. Eventually, the leadership of the company changed and with it came new energy and a thirst for fresh young talent. My dad could see the writing on the wall and transitioned to another smaller insurance company where he finished up his final years working. I remember him departing for work around eight in the morning and returning at five at night. This in no way sounds like the environment of today. Our global interconnectedness and the speed at which change comes, especially over the Internet, is staggering. My dad's situation, which was the norm, has now become the exception. Employees frequently change companies and careers and tend to move more often. For those who do plant roots, job security is not what it used to be. As I wrote this book, the economy seemed to be improving, but most remained skeptical. Start-up companies were appearing quite frequently, and new innovative ways of entering the market seemed to be the flavor of the day. Many companies are outsourcing much of their functions and technology is replacing jobs that used to be completed by the American worker. Still, amidst all this change, there is one constant, and I witnessed this as I visited numerous companies; people still exist in the modern workplace, and regardless of their job, require investment. As technology has replaced some jobs and arguably made our lives easier, it has also, in many ways, replaced interpersonal contact, which is so important. We may not have to physically hit print on the company printer or dial a phone to get a cab but now more than ever, in my opinion, we must connect as human beings. We must use the time and energy saved by smartphones to make a difference in those around us. A marketing specialist and a helicopter crew chief require investment just as my dad did in his job years ago. It's time to look away from the computer screen and into the eyes of another person.

There are no perfect organizations, mine included. If you can make a special connection with your team, you will be amazed at what happens. Think of the employee far away from you dealing with a disgruntled customer who does the right thing. Think about the employee who skips lunch or stays late at work because he or she knows the importance of their task to the success of the company. Think about the soldier far away from his or her base who steps in and stops his comrades from conducting an act that may lead to the death of innocent civilians. They do this because they know you have their back; you trust them and have created a healthy work environment that they deeply appreciate. These people will break through a wall for you and the organization. More importantly, these people will better people. This is the sweet spot. If by whatever means you choose, you can achieve this result, you have done your job as a leader. My hope is that this book contributes to your efforts in some way. You'll face naysayers, and you will hit obstacles. You may even be embarrassed as you expose your own vulnerabilities. The crisis of the day will chase you and attempt to take you from your people. However, you decide to proceed, overcome all that stands in your way. I cannot say how specifically your people will benefit, but I can promise this, they will benefit. You will too. Make it personal, not personnel. After all, it is personal, very personal. Good luck. Now go invest in your people!

ABOUT THE AUTHOR

Colonel Rob Campbell (USA, Retired) entered the Army in 1990 and served a 27-year career as an infantry officer, ranger and paratrooper, commanding infantry and cavalry units from platoon to brigade. Rob is a veteran of the wars in Iraq and Afghanistan and served during Hurricane Katrina relief efforts in New Orleans, Louisiana. After retiring in 2016, Rob began a consulting, coaching and speaking business through which he delivers his message about investing in people. He serves as an adjunct professor at the Marine Corps University and enjoys adventure motorcycle riding, the beach, reading and writing.

Rob is a native of Massachusetts and graduated from the Massachusetts College of Liberal Arts in North Adams, Massachusetts. He has master's degrees from Central Michigan University and the United States Army War College. Rob and his wife Leslie have two sons, Robbie and Louden, and have settled on the North Carolina coast. *It's Personal, Not Personnel* is Rob Campbell's first book.